SHADES OF BLUE

SHADES OF BLUE

FROM STREET COP TO POLICE CHIEF

Chief Joe Pelkington

To order additional copies of this book, contact:
Xlibris Corporation
1-888-795-4274
www.Xlibris.com
Orders@Xlibris.com
43025

CONTENTS

To all my fellow officers who looked death in the eyes and survived . . .

Never forget those who didn't.

This book is dedicated to the memory of our fallen comrades.

PREFACE

This book travels back to those dark days of segregation and the impending violence of the civil rights movement and the police lacking the experience and training to deal with it effectively. Included in this mix was the justice system of yesteryear that condoned broad discretion by police in the use of force, which by today's standards is unacceptable.

That era stimulated an upward evolutionary trend in police leadership brought on by society's extraordinary demands for professional police service and conduct, resulting in a greater level of police accountability.

Police humor, tragedy, violence, compassion, dedication, courage, and misconduct are all revealed in the following chapters. There are examples of incidents involving high-risk encounters by police and lawbreakers. By far, the greatest majority of men and women in the police profession are good, clean individuals that genuinely like helping people. They come from many different backgrounds, and for any number of reasons they decide to become police officers. Many times it's just a matter of job opportunity and economics, just needing a way to make a living.

But as they enter the field of law enforcement, they have a distinct change of attitude. Those who remain in this field of work are generally strongly opinionated about their personal and professional values, society, and the criminal justice system. One characteristic that may be latent at the onset of a police career but most likely develops as they join the ranks of their comrades, is a commitment that they make to themselves—silently. They will never shame the professional police image by failing to respond to a dangerous situation, one that is life threatening to them, a fellow officer, or a citizen. The thought and fear of paying the ultimate sacrifice is in all of us, but the thought and fear of failing our fellow police officers, or helpless human beings, is embedded in our hearts and minds. This is the sine qua non of a professional police officer.

ACKNOWLEDGMENT

To my fellow officers, other city of Treasure Island workers, friends, local citizens, business owners, waitresses, and so many more who encouraged me to write a book, all I can say is thanks for that encouragement.

I cannot say enough about my friend June Entwistle, a lady very much dedicated to teaching others to write. Her remarkable devotion to the literary field is second to none. She helped make this book possible.

And special thanks to Bonni Spivak, a true literary professional. Her knowledge and editorial expertise made the publication of this book a reality. I'll always be grateful for her encouragement, advice, patience, and providing me with invaluable knowledge.

During the several years, involving many hours night after night and weekends, dedicated to writing this book, my loving wife, Alice, provided great guidance, patience, and support in her review of the manuscript. Without her love and loyalty, this book would not have been possible. Thank you, sweetheart.

1

The Streets of Tampa

Why would anyone want to be a cop? It's dangerous work for low pay, stressful, and there is constant public and judicial scrutiny. A cop is loved and hated at the same time.

As a patrol sergeant on the midnight shift working the downtown area, one of my patrol units received a call to a skid row hotel. "Possible signal 7 (dead person) in room 112." It was almost daylight, and there was only about an hour to go before shift change. But if this was a confirmed death, it would take several hours to complete the investigation and much longer if foul play was suspected.

I was already in the sergeants' office, editing the shift's reports when the call went out.

When I arrived at the hotel, I climbed the stairs to the second floor. All these places were dingy and dark with a lingering musty odor. By this time in my career, I had experienced some death scenes that most people couldn't handle. A seasoned officer is conditioned to deal with death, but this one hurts. This death was different. This was the death of an infant Mexican girl whose parents were very young—the mother in her late teens and the father not much older. They embraced and were quietly crying. The officers handling the case were doing all they could to console them.

An opened dresser drawer took the place of a crib. The baby was lying face up inside. She was very clean, with a pillow in the drawer beneath her little body. A small baby blanket covered her up to the waist; thick, rich black hair surrounded her little round olive-skinned face, giving the appearance that she was sleeping peacefully.

I was so startled, I had to reach out and touch her beautiful but very cold face to be convinced she was dead. My officers' faces revealed they felt the pain, and we all had trouble staying composed. That was more than thirty-five years ago; and yet today, I still see that beautiful, peaceful little girl lying there in that drawer—a victim of sudden infant death syndrome or, as it was commonly called then, crib death.

*

One night, when I was still a rookie in training, my senior partner, Whitehurst, and I received a call to St. Joseph's Hospital emergency room. There we encountered an Irish-American family. Two small siblings were on oxygen and struggling to breath. One died just minutes after our arrival; the second child was hanging on to life by a thread.

The emergency room's medical staff was mystified as they tried to determine if this was the result of some type of poisoning. But the symptoms did not give clues to any antidote. An older sister and brother were instructed by the parents to drive home and bring back the rest of the younger children as the parents knew they were going to be at the hospital for quite some time. Minutes later, the adult siblings came rushing back into the emergency room with an unconscious six-year-old brother who died very soon after arriving.

As we watched helplessly, the emotion of this family's loss of one child was bad enough, but two of the youngest gone was one of the saddest incidents I've had to handle. I didn't sleep much that night.

We learned the next day that the children had been swinging on a rope hanging from a tree in their backyard, adjacent to an alleyway, which was stacked with trash for pickup. Apparently, the neighbors had discarded a burlap bag that contained a deadly insecticide: parathion. The kids had tied the burlap to the rope to hang on to while swinging. Because it was summer, they were not wearing any shirts, and the highly toxic insecticide was absorbed right into their bodies.

Dealing with death is common in police work. If you cannot control your emotions, this is not the job for you. You have to toughen up to function effectively on the street. Stress on the job hits everyone. The trick is to recognize and deal with it effectively. Many people just can't cope with the rigors of police work, and eventually they must change their profession or somehow get off the street and into an administrative position.

*

In the early 1960s, the patrol division was divided into three patrol areas citywide:

squad 1—downtown and Ybor City
squad 2—the east side and northeast Tampa area
squad 3—the west side and northwest Tampa area

I broke in on squad 1. This area was divided into three patrol zones:

downtown—zones 1 and 2 (both zones combined into one patrol uptown—zone 3
Ybor City—zone 4

There were five walking beats: beats 1 and 2 downtown, beat 3 (skid row) uptown, and beats 4 and 5 on Broadway (Seventh Avenue) in Ybor City. Each squad had one and two-man patrol units. In squad 1, zones 1 and 2 and 4 were two-man units. Only zone 3 was a one-man unit. The two-man units patrolled the more violent neighborhoods, and squad 1 covered one of the most violent areas in the city—a racially diverse area of blacks, whites, and Latinos.

*

After ten weeks of academy training, you're anxious to get on the street. I started on the evening swing shift—4:00 PM to midnight.

The old Tampa police station was built in early 1900s and located on the corner of Jackson Street and Florida Avenue. It was situated directly south of and behind City Hall. The buildings were linked together by an exterior second-floor walkway. There was no parking close to the police station, unless you wanted to feed a parking meter. Parking spaces were full during the day and evening shift hours, so we would park in the vicinity of Brorein Street, which was close to the police garage, about four blocks south of the police building.

On the last day at the police academy, we were told that instead of walking the distance, we could generally hitch a ride with one of the patrol or traffic units gassing up at the police garage before they returned to the station for shift change. It was standard practice to gas up just before parking in the alley behind the station and turning your cruiser over to your relief.

I arrived at the police garage about thirty minutes before roll call. I walked up to a small group of officers chatting at the gas pumps and asked if I could get a ride to the police station. A rather large officer, obviously older and seasoned, looked over at me for a few seconds and with a smirk that revealed his irritation said, "Fuck no, rookie. Take a walk." Several other officers smiled, chuckled, and drove off.

Approximately one year later, while on patrol downtown, I was dispatched to meet a traffic officer. Patrol and traffic were two separate divisions back then, and traffic units turned over violators, other than those being arrested for a traffic offense, to a patrol unit. The traffic officer was standing by with a drunken male.

When I arrived, the traffic officer motioned for me to take custody of the drunk he'd detained. I smiled because this was the same officer who had refused to give me a ride from the police garage on my first day on the job.

He looked somewhat puzzled when I said, "Fuck no, traffic man. Remember the rookie who asked for a ride to the police station?" I walked to my cruiser and left the scene.

*

I learned a lot that first year as a rookie. The City Hall complex was located on beat 1. You worked directly out of police headquarters when assigned walking beats 1 and 2. The day shift was, logically, the busiest of the shifts.

As in every sizable city, the downtown area was filled with hustle and bustle. Beat officers were always busy. Between vehicle and pedestrian traffic, there was always something happening that needed police attention.

Traffic backed up? The officer directed traffic and got that street cleared.

Pedestrian fell? Was there an injury? The officer needed to get an ambulance, write a report, and have a patrol unit follow up at the emergency room.

"Hey, Officer . . . that guy just stole a carton of cigarettes from my store." The beat officer chased him down, called for the paddy wagon, and wrote a report.

"Hey, Officer, some lady fainted over on Jackson Street." The officer ran over to assist, yelling, "Somebody needs to call police communications. Get an ambulance down here."

A citizen standing close by said, "I don't know the number."

The officer provided the phone number. "Hurry! She's not breathing!"

How different it is now. With modern technology, officers on foot carry portable radios and have immediate contact with emergency entities.

While you waited for emergency vehicles to show up, it seemed like twenty minutes went by when it was actually less than half that amount of time. When you were busy and couldn't get to the call box to call in on the hour, the police dispatcher alerted the downtown patrol unit to check the beat to make sure you were okay.

On the downtown beat, especially the day shift, you were always in the limelight. The mayor, city councilmen, the police chief, and high-profile business people traveled on foot, and you were constantly running into them somewhere while walking your beat.

They always liked to stop and talk to the police. You had to be ready to answer their questions. One thing you learned quickly was that when dealing with politicians, you had to be forthright but at the same time refrain from criticizing city or police department policies. No putdowns of other politicians, or anyone for that matter, even when it appeared the one you were dealing with was attempting to elicit your opinion to controversial questions. You always had to be the diplomat, be professional and neutral in your responses. The politician might have been annoyed when he didn't obtain the information that he asked for, but he would not forget your honesty and professional demeanor.

*

Starting out as a new officer, you are naturally self-conscious; it came with being the center of attraction. Police image is important. All eyes are constantly on the uniformed gun-toting officer, especially when events are happening and you're taking, or contemplating taking, some level of police action. "You're under arrest. Take your hands out of your pockets . . . Get out of the car . . . Everybody up on the sidewalk, please. Give the paramedics room to work."

Every move you make is being observed and recorded in someone's mind. An officer must be cognizant that he or she is being watched because any wrongdoing on the part of the officer is mostly what people remember. Of course, they also remember outstanding police action—a dramatic rescue or the apprehension of a thief. But it's the controversial things you do and the mistakes that you make that seem to stick in peoples' minds. And it's precisely those negative actions or observations that come back to haunt you. Sadly, some things you do are perceived negatively when you were, in fact, doing your job the way you were supposed to.

Anytime you're involved in a violent confrontation, your actions may become controversial and all too frequently may be portrayed unfairly by the news media.

The news media cuts and pastes your actions and often presents police conduct in a bad light because it generates sensationalism on the evening TV news and in hardcopy headlines. However, those media folks have deadlines and are constantly under pressure to get the story and get it in on time for the news hour or hard print for the morning news. Frequently, there just isn't sufficient time to get all the facts. While the role of the press is critical in ferreting out government wrongdoing, you have to suspect, at times, they extemporize because of the pressure to meet deadlines.

I recall an event during the 1960s civil rights movement involving two officers scuffling with a very large black female. The front page of a national magazine illustrated two officers in a large city, one on each side of a black female. She was grimacing and down on her knees with her hands positioned over her head as if to protect herself from being struck by one of the officers holding a nightstick (baton) in both hands. In the photo, it appeared that the officer intended to strike her on the head. The other officer also had a grimace on his face with his hands clenched just above the woman's head as if he too was about to strike her.

As police officers viewing this photograph on the magazine cover, we were bewildered. How could two officers be brutalizing the woman like that? We had no answer, but another version of the story eventually filtered down to police agencies throughout the nation. Apparently, the black female, scuffling with the officers, gained control of the nightstick. Both officers grabbed the nightstick, pulled it up, and had just regained control when the picture was taken. The photo showing the position of the nightstick in the one officer's hands, the position of the other officer' s hands and the position of the black female's hands would lead anyone to logically believe those officers were about to hit what appeared to be a defenseless female who was on her knees.

You had to believe the media people responsible for allowing these photos to be published knew very well what the logical perception of the public would be. Is it any wonder that the police distrust the media?

*

While the traditional police hat is viewed as instant recognition of a police officer's presence, for the patrol officer, many times it was a hindrance because of the preoccupation of putting it on and taking it off.

In those days, the only time you could appear without wearing your uniform hat was in a bathroom, a church, or when sitting inside a restaurant eating. Once, when I was still a fairly new officer, I was assigned to beat 1 on the day shift. I was walking along Florida Avenue when I stopped in front of a hotel and nodded good morning to the doorman.

Directly across Florida Avenue, there was a bus stop right in front of a church with a dozen or more people waiting for the bus. The benches were full, and the others were standing. So my self-consciousness kicked in and making an attempt to look casual, I lit up a cigarette. Many of us smoked back then. I stepped forward to prop my foot up on what appeared to be a metal post. It turned out to be a *rubber* post painted gunmetal gray. I leaned forward, placing my foot on the post, and of course, my body tilted and kept going until I lost my balance. My hat fell off into the street, and I was close behind.

I picked up my hat and dusted it off, trying desperately not to look across at the people waiting at the bus stop. But failing in that, my peripheral vision picked up shaking and laughter from my audience. Fortunately, the noisy traffic drowned out the sound of the laughter. I looked over at the doorman, and if he didn't begin to laugh soon, his head would have definitely exploded. I did my best to move on with some dignity.

*

In another incident, earlier in my first year on the job, I had the opportunity to get my feet wet on my first traffic control assignment. One summer Sunday afternoon, the police dispatcher directed my partner and me to Dale Mabry Highway and Hillsborough Avenue to direct traffic. Both roadways were state roads and very heavily traveled, especially on weekends when people drove west to the gulf beaches in the early part of the day and came back east in the late afternoon. Traffic was backed up for a mile or more, and the traffic light couldn't handle it all. My partner took advantage of his seniority, dumped me out at the intersection, and drove off laughing. There I was, with traffic backed up in every direction as far as the eye could see.

I had no way to shut off the traffic light as I didn't have a key to the traffic control box. I stood there stunned, wondering how the hell I was going to get out in the middle of the intersection and control the traffic. After a moment of wondering, I decided I had to do something, so I made it to the middle of the intersection directly under the traffic light. But I now couldn't use the light in my efforts to direct traffic because I couldn't see it.

I took a deep breath and placed the metal whistle in my mouth, intending to blow hard and stop traffic flowing eastbound. But I was so nervous when I blew the whistle it catapulted onto the pavement in front of me. I made a hasty attempt to retrieve it by bending over and reaching for it when my hat fell off. One car flattened the whistle. Another car flattened my hat. No hat, no whistle, no directing traffic. When my partner returned he had a good laugh. Only because of my military training and discipline did I refrain from making any insubordinate remarks.

*

One night, when I was a patrol sergeant, I was insubordinate to my superior officers in an incident involving the wearing of the police hat. I responded to assist one of my officers making an arrest at a traffic stop. When I arrived, I could see the officer struggling with the suspect. A pretty good-sized man stood there who did not take kindly to the free room and board that was being offered to him at the city jail. We tussled with this guy for a few minutes, rolling around on the street very close to moving traffic.

When we finally succeeded in getting him handcuffed, we were both winded and dirty with blood splattered on our uniforms, some of it ours. Just about the time we secured the prisoner in the patrol car, the Captain and his lieutenant drove up.

Now you have to know something about these two. They really weren't interested in doing any work or in getting their hands dirty. This kind of supervisors and commanders were limited to functioning well within written rules and procedures. God help anyone who stepped outside the rules even when a unique situation would justify it.

They drove within twenty-five feet of us, and when the captain motioned me over to their car, I was still trying to straighten out my uniform. He demanded to know why I wasn't wearing my hat. Still catching my breath, I pointed to my officer, also winded and nursing a cut hand. Then I pointed to our hats on the ground close to the patrol car. I paused and said, "Unless you have some interest in what happened in this case, then I would like to get my hat and clean it before wearing it. Do you have any other stupid fucking questions?" I walked away without waiting for an answer.

I automatically assumed I'd be disciplined for my outburst, but I really didn't give two shits about it. It seemed that a few commanders are always perched on their asses, thinking of ways to screw with the troops and changing anything they could just to say they did something. God forbid they should screw up themselves and admit they made a mistake.

In any case, I was saved from disciplinary action only because these two were not about to show up their own asses by submitting a disciplinary report to the division commander that while fighting a suspect, our hats fell off!

*

One night, standing before four squads of officers and their sergeants, I apologized for a decision I made the night before. No real harm was done, but it just happened to be the wrong decision. There was dead silence—they were stunned.

Later, while working in my office, the sergeants came in, and one of them said, "You know, Lieutenant, what you did tonight by apologizing earned you a lot of respect from our officers.

If commanders would stop and think about it, they have no qualms about disciplining officers when they make a mistake. When a supervisor makes a mistake, even the most disconnected officer knows it!

President Kennedy visits Tampa Nov. 1963—
Tampa Police Escort Team

TPD—CIRCA EARLY 1900s

Circa—1915/1961

2

The Acid Test

After a successful field training program, a new officer is assigned to work a patrol zone. This is the acid test for the officer. Now he's alone in a patrol car, answering calls, conducting traffic stops, and making his or her own decisions. It's during this period that rookie officers must prove their worth as street cops. All eyes are on the new guy to see if he has what it takes.

*

My first night working solo held an unplanned surprise as I wasn't scheduled to be out in the field alone. When I reported for midnight shift duty, I learned that my senior partner, the field training officer, had called in sick, so Sergeant D. G. Neal decided it was time to turn me loose on my own.

It was a cool, clear Florida winter night. Most of the time on weekdays, after the bars closed, it was relatively quiet. Surprisingly, I wasn't a bit nervous. I was more excited, eager, and watchful, listening to every police radio transmission that blared out into the quiet night air.

Halfway through the shift, I was stopped at the traffic light headed southbound on Tampa Street at Columbus Drive. No traffic flowed in any direction. When the light turned green and I started to cross the intersection, a car with no headlights on blew the red light, going westbound on Columbus Drive. It missed me by just a few feet. I estimated his speed at about seventy to eighty miles per hour. I took chase and advised the dispatcher I had one running westbound on Columbus Drive. I was only able to catch up with him because he slowed down, circled around, and headed south on Tampa Street.

My first chase! I wheeled the cruiser with one hand and kept the dispatcher informed of my location and direction of travel with the microphone that I held in the other hand. Was I nervous? Oh, yeah! The guy raced through downtown and over the bridge onto Davis Island.

Davis Island is a maze of circling streets with names I'd never seen or heard before. I chased this crazy bastard through winding residential streets while the dispatcher screamed at me wanting—no, demanding—my location and direction of travel. I didn't know who was pissed off more—the dispatcher or me.

Sliding around corners, mailboxes going down, the damn spiral radio microphone cord I was holding in my right hand wrapped around the steering post while I tried to use both hands to turn the wheel. The microphone fell between my legs, swinging back and forth and banging the hell out of both my knees. By now, the dispatcher was frantically screaming over the radio. This I didn't need. All I wanted to do was to catch this guy and operate on his head with my nightstick. Just ten seconds—that's all I needed.

The chase ended abruptly when he slammed his car into a pole. The suspect then tried desperately to climb out the window of the car. As I approached him, all I could hear was the dispatcher screaming over and over again, "ZONE 3 WHAT'S YOUR 10-20 [location]!" All I knew was that I was somewhere on Davis Island. Using both hands, I grabbed the suspect by the shirt collar. Already shook up from the accident, he hung halfway out the car window. Meanwhile, the dispatcher was still screaming, and I still didn't know my location.

I was pissed off and yelled at the suspect, "Where the hell are we?"

In a sobbing voice, he said, "I don't know."

Finally, a resident, standing in pajamas outside his front door, calmly gave me our exact location. Thank you. When I turned in my report, the only question my sergeant had for me was why I didn't communicate with the dispatcher.

*

During my first year on probation, I learned quickly about dealing with violent people. Police officers work in an environment that, at times, demands quick action.

On the street, your partner is your best friend. But working alone, one-man units always back each other up on calls that have the potential for danger. One of the greatest risks is an officer's self-initiating action based on what he observes and investigates while on patrol; therefore, you are wise to size up every situation you may encounter. The most seemingly benign incident could be a blind date with death.

Once working a day shift, I responded to a disturbance call at a run-down motel on the upper east side of town. When I arrived, the complainant pointed out the troublemaker—a white male who was walking away. When I ordered him to stop, he quickly looked back and then continued walking away. I followed him to a general store.

I stepped in, intending to confront this guy. He walked to the rear of the store where a number of other redneck types were standing around a potbellied stove.

Sizing up the situation, it was obvious he had allies. Knowing the attitude of these locals and that my backup was on the way, I stepped back, ordered a soda from the clerk, and waited. My backup was a motorcycle traffic cop, Ed Wonka, at that time a man much more experienced than I was.

When Ed got there, we approached the suspect, escorted him outside, searched him, and found a putty knife in the utility slot of his bib overalls. It was honed down to razor sharpness. This guy was wanted for assaulting a county deputy, and he had a history of violence, especially against police officers. So, *sizing up* a situation is simply good thinking.

*

At some point, once you'd proven yourself, you were assigned to skid row—a walking beat. Skid row, lined with small taverns, cheap hotels, and a few used clothes and shoe stores stretched approximately six blocks, beginning at the northern end of downtown Tampa.

The row always had a familiar stench that hung in the air. When you stepped into the drab-looking bars along the row, they reeked of cigarette smoke, and the streets and sidewalks were always in need of repair. Discarded empty cigarette packs, cigarette butts, empty beer cans and pint-sized liquor bottles littered the gutter and vestibules of closed storefronts.

Standing at the northern end of the beat looking south, you watched the occasional drunk pop his head out the entrance of a bar, checking if the beat officer was close by. Spotting the officer, the drunk would quickly duck back inside; back then, drunks were arrested when officers came across them.

*

On a busy summer weekend night, with the bars' doors all open, the beat officer could hear loud laughter and the incessant chatter of drinking patrons lined up along the bars, waving their arms around to emphasize a point or to tell their stories. I walked the skid row beat for a year. There were three call boxes on the beat, one at each end and one in the middle, with a direct phone line to police communications.

The downtown two-man patrol car would periodically drive along the row, especially on the night shift, to check up on the beat man. They also wanted to find out if he had arrested any drunks. Officers making an arrest had to appear in court the next morning on their own time.

Once you made your first arrest and the patrol units in the area heard the police dispatcher sending you the paddy wagon, they knew you had to go to court in the morning and would bring all the drunks they arrested during the shift down to skid row so you could testify in court that they were, in fact, drunk. Then the beat man was the arresting officer, and the other officers didn't have to appear in court. This was not really a problem because you didn't walk skid row without making arrests, no matter which shift you worked.

That meant if you worked the evening shift, you got off at midnight and had to be back in city court at 9:00 AM. So why should everybody have to go to court if one officer could do it all? What the hell, you had court anyway, right?

It all sounded good until you got to court with your pink arrest slips on the five or six arrests you had made. But wait—on the docket you had fifteen arrests. Where the hell did they come from? Well, if the beat man was going to court anyway, other officers just put his name on their pink arrest slips. The problem was that these guys never brought the drunks by for me to see so I could truthfully testify, "Yes, Your Honor. He was drunk."

But the old judge knew the game. He would line up the drunks and say, "If you plead guilty, you get ten days in the city stockade. But plead not guilty and if you are convicted, it's the officer's word against a drunk's, you get thirty days." Guess how many drunks pleaded not guilty.

*

On skid row, the drunks paid no attention to the time of day. Your chance of running into a problem was the same, day or night.

In those days, most Floridians had never heard of a Chinese restaurant, much less ever seen one. But there was one at the northern end of skid row. The owner was not Asian but sure tried to look the part, Fu Manchu mustache and all. I can't remember the name of the restaurant now, but wrestlers liked hanging out there.

One day while I was walking the beat, the owner yelled out the door, "Hey! Help! They're tearing up my place."

Two huge wrestlers were drunk and fighting. There I was between two extra-large-sized professional wrestlers, grasping each of them by the arm and walking—or should I say trying to walk—them across Franklin Street to the call box.

When a skinny cop tried to haul two wrestlers with a combined weight of over five hundred pounds across a street, it stopped traffic. Pedestrians looked at us with a combination of amusement and awe, not really believing what they were seeing.

The wrestlers begged me to let them go, and realizing their pleas were falling on deaf ears, they then begin stuffing money into any of my uniform pockets they could reach. Considering a police officer's meager salary in those days, it must have been a tremendous temptation for (thankfully) a very few officers.

An officer's salary did not begin to cover all his expenses, much less allow him to be able to afford to eat out, buy a new car, a bigger home, or a college education. Many of us couldn't have survived without a trip to the credit union every three or four months to add more to our perpetual outstanding loan just to pay the bills.

Trying to negotiate these two gladiators across the street in traffic while they attempted to stuff money in my pockets (to the amusement of pedestrians and shop owners) was a feat not recorded in any almanac.

Encounters with professional wrestlers were a unique situation. They were, of course, very powerful and solid as rocks. They knew very well they could take down a cop. But they were also aware of an officer's ability to employ the use of his firearm for self-defense.

In the case of dealing with wrestlers, there was no debate. The only way to prevent a wrestler from inflicting serious injury was employing your firearm. Today, there's the pepper spray and Taser, commonly referred to as a stun gun. When fired, they deliver a whopping 50,000 volts via two wire leads that attach themselves to the suspect's body. They deliver no amps, however, so they do not cause any serious injury. These devices are very effective, and even though there is controversy regarding those rare cases resulting in deaths, the cause was determined to be from some sort of violent delirium brought on by excessive alcohol and/or drug use, not the use of the Taser.

Overall, I believe statistics will confirm the use of the Taser by the police in violent and potentially violent encounters has reduced injury and death of both police officers and suspects. But as usual, there are those naysayers, the antipolice folks in our society who insist the use of force by the Taser, pepper spray, etc., is killing people. WHAT ABOUT GUNS! Will that be the next opposition waged against police?

One afternoon, a humorous incident with a wrestler occurred in Ybor City. His first name was Charlie, and he was well-known for clearing out a bar if someone pissed him off while he was drinking. On this day, Charlie ran his car off Broadway into a vacant lot, coming to a stop against the brick wall of a multistory building.

He had struck the building at a forty-five degree angle with the left front fender of his car smashed against the wall. I was working zone 3 on patrol when I heard the call go out. Not being busy, I was headed that way when I heard the beat officer tell the police dispatcher that he had arrived on the scene.

When I arrived, the young beat officer and another patrol officer, neither too long out of the academy, just stood there looking at Charlie, who ignored their order to get out of the car. The driver's door was half opened against the wall. Sizing up the situation, it was apparent I would have to take the initiative even though it was not my call and could have simply driven off.

I approached the car, and Charlie, still sitting behind the wheel, looked up at me when I said a friendly hello.

Trying to inject some humor into a tense situation, I said, "Hey, Charlie, you sure body slammed the station wagon."

After a while, I finally coaxed him out. Charlie was built like a beer barrel, and when he stood up, all three hundred plus pounds of him pressed me against the wall. Charlie smiled—I smiled, and in a weak, strained whisper I said, "Charlie, I can't breathe." Fortunately, he didn't offer any resistance and cooperated in his arrest. Charlie proved to be good-natured, or at least he was that day. Thank you for that.

*

The walking beat was tough on my feet. Yes, they were already flat when I hired on. Back then you bought your own shoes. The only equipment the department supplied was the badge, collar brass, and uniforms. You had to buy everything else: gun, leather gear, handcuffs, nightstick, flashlight, and any other equipment you needed or wanted. I would go to the old army or navy surplus store, buy a pair of navy last black low quarters for six dollars and suffer through a two week break-in period.

Most cops who walked the skid row beat became friendly with the bar owners. Some officers took free cigarettes—I didn't. A few even patronized the bars after duty hours. I gave fair consideration to both merchants and vagrants. Just because some poor guy was down and out or an alcoholic didn't mean he should be treated with less respect than anyone else.

*

One night a farmer from the rural area of Hillsborough County, bib overalls, straw hat and all—found me on the beat, saying "they" had stolen his brand-new watch at the Saratoga Bar. He said he had bought some guy a drink because he was friendly, but when he tried to leave, the bar owner told him, "You owe me fifty dollars for buying everybody in the bar drinks." He didn't have the money, so the bar owner took his new watch instead. He had just bought the watch that day after selling his produce in town.

I told the bar owner to give back the man's wristwatch. The owner refused.

I then asked, "What time is it?"

"Nine-thirty," said the owner.

I said, "Say, it's Friday night. How late do you stay open? Till about 3:00 AM, right?" He nodded yes. "You really make good money on Friday nights, right?"

"Yeah," said the owner.

I went on, "Well, how much are you going to make if I call the paddy wagon down here and load up every thirty minutes?"

The farmer got his watch back.

Later that morning, after the shift was over, I had to report to the captain's office. He directed me to never threaten a bar owner like that again.

I said, "No, sir, I won't. Next time, I'll just lock him up for theft."

The captain was not very happy with me. I still believe that attitude cost me corporal stripes. It took several more years for me to get them.

*

Most of the people on skid row were alcoholics and homeless—in essence, vagrants. Most, however, were not bad or mean people. I only locked up those who could not take care of themselves or were just troublemakers. If they had a room in a flophouse, I helped them to the room if I wasn't busy. I even let those without a room sleep in alleys and other niches on the row. More than once I bought some of them coffee or food. I figured they were in worse shape than I was when it came to money.

When I started with the department, money was scarce. A police officer's salary was only $4,000 annually. No overtime pay. I worked part-time as an auto mechanic and painted houses in addition to doing off-duty police jobs to make ends meet. For me, any assignment on the midnight shift was murder. I worked all day then worked all night. Usually I only got about four or five hours sleep.

Some of the skid row guys got in tight with me. My theory was if I took care of some of the good ones, then they would look out for me. Those I thought I could trust with a call box key were told, "If you ever see me getting my ass kicked, get to the call box and call for help."

You know, it worked. Twice while on duty on the row, I needed help and that's how I got it.

There were several skid row guys who possessed special skills. One had been an accountant, another had been a professional baseball player, and another, a very good chef. Some of them received a monthly social security check. They cashed it, then would drink up, they'd be arrested and spend time in the city stockade, then they'd get out, get the next check, cash it—the cycle continued.

City prisoners could work off their time. One day's work took three days off their sentences. While incarcerated, the accountant took care of the stockade's books. The chef worked his time off cooking for the other prisoners. Often, the stockade captain would call down to the station and say go find so-and-so and arrest him. We need him to balance the books, or we need a cook this week.

Some of those who had a key to the call box would call police communications and ask for the paddy wagon, especially in colder months. They wanted to go to the stockade. They would get free room and board, medical attention, and a chance to dry out. I had one guy following me around, practically begging to be arrested.

When I said, "I can't arrest you if you're not violating the law," he took a swing at me.

He got his wish.

*

One night at about 2:00 or 3:00 AM, while patrolling downtown, my partner and I were parked just north of skid row, writing reports when a vagrant walked up and told us a guy carrying a brick was on the row looking for the beat man. He said that when he found him, he was going to ambush the guy for putting him in jail.

We headed for skid row, looking for both the suspect and the beat officer. We found and approached the suspect on foot, ordering him to drop the brick. He turned toward us without uttering a word with a menacing look on his face. He advanced on us, and we took him down after knocking the brick from his hand with a nightstick. This guy was serious.

For a vagrant to alert us was not uncommon. Most of these people weren't bad, just down-on-their-luck alcoholics and in some cases, mentally ill. Of course, in their minds, helping us meant that just maybe we would give them a break in the future; and sometimes we did.

*

While I was walking the beat one relatively quiet night, a guy approached me and complained that someone was up in his bed in a skid row flophouse. When I got there, a drunk was passed out across the bed. I got him on his feet and walked him to the call box, calling for the paddy wagon. I charged him with vagrancy, a violation that usually carried a thirty-day stint in the city stockade. The guy was somewhat hung over but not giving me a hard time. The paddy wagon was busy, so the downtown patrol car arrived to transport my prisoner.

The senior officer, L. E. Young, frisked the prisoner and placed him in the backseat.

When L. E. started to leave, this guy waved his fist at me and said, "When I get out of the stockade, I'm going to kick your fucking rookie ass." Well, I was somewhat surprised but amused, and I laughed.

L.E., meanwhile, got out of the car, opened the rear cruiser door, pulled the guy to a standing position in front of me, and told him, "Why wait? Do it now." And he drove off.

Now I was really surprised. The guy was wide eyed and stunned, not believing what had just happened. He glanced up at me with a terrified look, dropped to his knees, and started to cry. In the meantime, L. E., who had circled the block, pulled back up.

He asked, "Hey, tough guy, how come the rookie is still standing up?"

Back in the cruiser, he went, and quietly, off to jail.

3

Response to Violent Incidents

If the sight of blood bothers you, forget about a career as a police officer.

Sunday mornings are usually the quietest time on patrol, but there are exceptions. Assigned to zone 3 one Sunday morning, I responded to a stabbing in zone 4 on Twenty-second Street in Ybor City because the zone 4 patrol unit was busy handling another call.

When I arrived on the scene, the paramedics were loading a badly cut up black man in his eighties. He had been doing what he does every day, sitting in front of a grocery store, talking and telling stories. He was a kindly old gentleman, well liked by everyone in the neighborhood. A black male in his forties had walked up, and for no apparent reason, repeatedly stabbed the old man then fled down a side street.

When I turned the corner in search of the suspect, I found that about forty or fifty people had chased and cornered him on the front porch of a house about two blocks from the crime scene.

Getting there quickly, I jumped up on the porch and positioned myself between the angry crowd and the suspect. People were screaming, "Kill the m—f—er."

The suspect, still in possession of the bloody knife, was backed up against the wall. He couldn't get by me or the crowd. I had called for backup before leaving the cruiser but wasn't sure I could contain the angry surging mob. They repeatedly ignored my order to calm down and stay back.

I drew my revolver, alternately pointing it at the threatening mob and then at the suspect who was wide-eyed and sweating profusely. He was like a cornered animal, still holding the knife, ignoring my repeated warnings to drop it. I saw him panic and try to bolt past me, in spite of my threat to shoot him. I then had to make a split-second decision about whether or not to shoot. Sizing up the suspect, I holstered my weapon and grabbed for his knife hand when he made a halfhearted attempt to strike out at me. I managed to grab his knife hand, and just at that moment, I spotted the backup unit, and the mob's encroachment waned.

We cuffed the suspect and quickly transported him out of the area. Fortunately, I only received a small but deep cut on the palm of my right hand. It should have been sutured, but back in those days, unless you were really hurt, you didn't bother with minor injuries.

As I was getting off duty later, I learned the old man had died. I had only seen him briefly when he was being treated by paramedics at the scene. I felt bad. The suspect, angry for some unknown reason, took his hostility out on the old man.

*

On another Sunday morning, the captain was conducting the roll call when police communications advised of a reported stabbing in progress in the area of Nebraska Avenue and Twiggs Street. The captain ordered my partner, Stout*, and me to respond. Officer Stout was a large man—not tall, just large. From the rear, you could look at the back of his head, and you could not distinguish it from his neck.

This area was a combination of a black neighborhood and run-down industrial buildings and abandoned shacks, a haven for hobos and drunks to take refuge.

Keep in mind, at this time in our nation's history, the South was still segregated. Black neighborhoods presented a different culture that required learning how to interact with angry people and understanding that many black citizens didn't trust the police, considering us the enemy. Arguments, domestic and otherwise, frequently resulted in violent fights with knives and guns. Rarely did witnesses come forward or provide any information to assist in an investigation.

In this case, however, when we arrived in the area, various people pointed down the street. We searched the area on foot, checking the vacant shacks. I approached a shack that stood behind another, one you might not immediately spot if it was dark.

Once inside, I could hear movement and observed a black male lying on his side, his back to me with his hands in front of his body. He appeared to be in his fifties or perhaps even older. When I approached him, he turned in my direction.

His light blue work shirt and both hands were soaked in blood. It took several seconds for me to realize he was attempting to stuff his entrails back into his abdominal cavity. The abdominal wound was huge. Dropping down, I placed both my hands against his and applied as much pressure as possible to control the bleeding. I yelled for my partner to call for paramedics.

The man was in great pain. He kept repeating in a weakened painful tone, "Please help me, Officer. Please help me." The paramedics arrived and took over, and the man survived.

I returned to the station, and the captain spotted me changing my bloody shirt.

*

Immediately after going back in service, we were dispatched to another stabbing just north of the police station on Highland Avenue. At the crime scene, a two-story house, paramedics were getting ready to load up a thirty-five-year-old black male into the ambulance. He'd suffered multiple stab wounds about his face, neck, and chest. It looked bad, but they always do, and we were always surprised when the victims survived. The human body is amazingly durable. Even with a great loss of blood, victims of such violence often manage to survive. And yet, at other times, a single nonimpressive stab wound is fatal. You just never know.

Walking up the exterior wooden stairs, we noticed blood splattered all the way to the second floor apartment. The front door remained closed.

Continuing to head up the stairs, we could hear the suspect, a very thin black female, cussing and refusing to come to the rickety screen door that separated her from our custody intentions. She continued to refuse to open the door despite Stout's repeated demands. A black male sitting on the couch refused to get involved.

Finally, I told Officer Stout to pull the screen door open. For whatever reason, he wouldn't do that. I then leaned over his shoulder and ripped it open. As we entered to make the arrest, Stout grabbed the suspect who then began to struggle. Now she was between us. I tried to handcuff her, but Stout, all two hundred thirty pounds of him, decided to push her out the door.

The female fought, and I slid backwards out the screen door and up against the rickety wooden railing on the outside staircase. I yelled for Stout to stop pushing her, but the woman still fought, and he continued to push her toward me.

At this point, I was still pressed against the railing, which was clearly not going to hold up. Twenty-five feet below me was a cement driveway, and it appeared that's where I was headed. I'm usually not one to strike a woman, but I swiftly punched her on the side of the head, and she tumbled down the entire flight of stairs, landing face up on the ground.

I ran down the stairs and knelt beside her. At first, there was no movement. Then in the next second, she wrapped herself around me like an Indian blanket. Stout sat on her, she was handcuffed, and headed for booking.

I was covered in blood, so it was back to the locker room to change my uniform shirt again, less than an hour after I had originally changed it. The captain saw me for the second time, covered in blood and changing my uniform shirt. He said nothing, just looked at me for a moment, then left.

*

One night on patrol, I heard an officer in an adjacent patrol zone advise the police dispatcher that he was going 10-50 (stopping a vehicle for traffic violation or investigation). He indicated it appeared he had a drunk driver. I quickly headed over to assist.

Arriving at the scene, I spotted Officer Franz Warner leaning against his cruiser with his head bent down toward the ground. The driver of the stopped car was still behind the wheel, which was unusual because drunks are removed from their cars as soon as possible. I could see Franz was upset.

"Hey, Franz, what's wrong?" I asked. He responded by shaking his head and pointing to the driver.

I could now see blood splattered on the opened car door window, steering wheel, and the driver's left hand, which rested on the car door. He was conscious, with his head bent slightly down toward his lap. I poked him lightly on the shoulder with my flashlight; and when he turned to look up at me, I saw that his face, neck, and the front of his shirt were all soaked in blood. I then reached to open the car door to determine how badly he was hurt. When the driver tried to talk to me, I heard a gurgling sound, and blood splattered all around his face and on me.

A closer look revealed something I hadn't seen before. There was a three-inch gash under his chin—and his tongue was protruding down through the gash so that when he tried to talk, his tongue flopped around, spraying blood in every direction.

The paramedics arrived within a few minutes. As it turned out, the wound was the result of a barroom brawl. The other guy, using a broken beer bottle, jammed the jagged edge upward under the victim's chin.

Even the paramedics were taken back by this man's wound. As they loaded him in the ambulance, I could see one medic was doing all he could to remain composed.

I was trying to comprehend the frame of mind of his assailant. What could have made someone so angry they would resort to inflicting such a wound? Then again, as I gained more experience, I learned just how vicious humans can be. Finding human body parts, including hands, heads, and fingers, gives you an idea of what vicious people are capable of doing to other humans.

*

This next case was one of the bloodiest I have ever heard of. Working the day shift, officers received a call to an apartment complex in a black neighborhood. The only information provided was that for about thirty minutes prior, neighbors had heard a consistent thumping noise, like someone falling repeatedly on the floor. Upon arrival, the officers knocked on the apartment door, but there was no response. They made several more attempts to gain admittance, but still no response. While interviewing the neighbors, the officers themselves heard the noise.

Now there was a reason to believe they might have had an emergency and possibly a victim in need of medical attention. Forcing open the locked door, they stepped into a pool of blood. Taken aback somewhat, both officers looked around and all they could see were pools of blood on the floor from the front door all the way back to the rear of the apartment into the kitchen. It was unbelievable.

Walking carefully, the officers searched the apartment, following the intermittent thumping noise. Reaching the back bedroom, they observed a man and a woman, both armed with butcher knives, tangled together doing the best they could to continue stabbing each other. No talking, yelling, cussing—not a word from either of them, just an incessant effort to bury their respective knives into each other's bodies.

The officers separated them and called for paramedics. They were both so saturated in blood it was difficult to determine how many wounds there were and where they were.

They never lost consciousness, nor did either say a word to the officers or each other. For a while, the officers actually thought that the man and the woman were mute. Finally, they responded to the request for their names. They were a husband and a wife in their fifties. The officers never learned why they were trying to kill each other, but it was another amazing case of survival.

*

Domestic violence is responsible for a significant number of the violent crimes nationwide. Many women are murdered at the hands of an abusive spouse or boyfriend. While husbands and boyfriends do occasionally become domestic murder victims themselves, the statistics pale in comparison to the murders of girlfriends, wives, and ex-wives.

While most domestic disputes never go beyond verbal arguments and minor assault injuries, it is a national concern and the justice system must be aggressive in its efforts to curtail and prevent further violence.

As it stands now, domestic violence disturbances are one of the most frequent types of incidents patrol officers respond to. One afternoon, a patrol unit responded to a domestic disturbance. The dispatcher advised that a female had called the police.

A small black female, about sixty years old, met the officers at the front door. They noted she had one eye swollen shut, and her face was covered in blood.

Before officers could say anything, she said, "He ain't gonna rap on me no mo'. I's tired of da beat'ns. No mo' beat'ns." Tears were streaming down her face.

Entering the front door, turning the corner into the foyer, the officers observed a black male lying face up on the couch. Buried in his throat was a long-handled axe. That small woman had whacked him so hard that only about two inches of the axe blade were visible above the surface of his neck. Blood had run down the side of the couch and covered an area of about three square feet.

The lady said, "All dem years he beat me, ebby day, comin' home drunk, and beat on me. But no mo', Officers, no mo'."

Seeing this incident, you truly had to feel sorry for her, no matter what her crime. Family members of the wife and even several neighbors apparently supported her claim of being constantly battered by her husband for more than "thirty years."

You had to wonder how she didn't kill him long before this.

There were numerous discussions about this case among officers, wondering if the lady would get probation as she was the true victim in this case. If there was ever such a thing as a delayed case of self-defense, this killing was it.

*

My partner and I responded to another incident, this time to the Tampa General Hospital emergency room with regard to an aggravated assault. Entering the emergency room, we heard the person we believed to be the victim speaking. He described being cut while at the same time shooting his attacker. The victim was a forty-five-year-old white male, about six feet four, lean, and a military veteran. The slashing knife wounds across his throat would have led you to believe that he should have bled to death. But the doctor, who was also surprised, said the jugular vein had somehow been spared. One more swipe with the knife and our victim could've been DOA at the hospital. Instead, he continued to ramble on about how he was attacked and why.

"I don't understand how that son of a bitch didn't go down. I shot him at least three times with a semiautomatic pistol at point-blank range. All the time I'm shooting him, he's not even fazed and kept right on stabbing me."

Based on his description of the incident, we were also puzzled. It would seem at such close range there would be sufficient force to disable the suspect. To add to the amazement, the victim described his assailant as about five feet six and no more than one hundred thirty pounds.

After completing our interview of the victim, we left the hospital, intending to visit the crime scene and look for physical evidence. As we walked out of the emergency room, a white male fitting the description of our stabbing suspect was walking up the ramp. His tee shirt was soaked in blood.

Spotting us, he said, "I'm the one you're looking for." He lifted up his shirt and displayed what appeared to be three bullet holes just below his chest area and corresponding exit wounds on his back. Once he was secured, we proceeded to the crime scene.

That's where the mystery was solved! Unbeknownst to our victim, the projectiles were *armor-piercing* bullets. The rounds sliced through

43

the suspect like a knife, but not one round struck a vital organ. If they had, more than likely he would not have survived. Searching the crime scene, we discovered that the armor-piercing rounds traveled straight through a window of the house and were embedded in tree trunks in the direct line of fire.

The reason for the altercation? Our victim was screwing the suspect's estranged wife. The suspect, drunk, was watching the house and broke into the bedroom—armed with a butcher knife he retrieved from the kitchen and attacked the victim. The victim knew the pistol was in the bedside end table because the suspect's wife had previously shown it to him, saying it belonged to another gentleman she was then seeing. You might say our victim got a bigger bang out of that evening than he bargained for, and the estranged wife wasn't the only one penetrated.

4

Burglary

Burglary is defined as entering or remaining in a dwelling, structure, or a conveyance with the intent to commit an offense therein, unless the premises are at the time open to the public or the defendant is licensed or invited to enter or remain there.

*

When I was a division commander (rank of major), one of my shift commanders, Captain Hatcher, and I went for lunch one afternoon. On the way back to the station, we heard patrol units conversing on the police radio. They were apparently trying to chase down a burglary suspect.

The suspect was successful in keeping his distance, and the patrol units lost sight of him in a neighborhood southwest of Highland and Buffalo avenues.

Almost in direct line with our route back to the station, we swung down Highland and observed officers hastily looking for the suspect in backyards and alleyways. We pulled up to where several officers, as well as a sergeant and lieutenant stood wondering where to look next.

We parked and approached them. They watched us walk past them and look under a house. We simultaneously yelled out, "Get out here now." They laughed—until we reached under the side of the house and pulled the suspect out by his feet. Officers immediately rushed back and handcuffed the suspect, looking at the captain and me in awe and as we continued walking toward our car, I smiled and said, "You're welcome."

It's not too often the troops see the brass get involved. I always enjoyed doing so. I guess it's because when I was a patrol officer, it was rare to see a commander anywhere on the street.

*

Assigned with my training officer one night to patrol zone 3, I was just a rookie still learning how to decipher police radio jargon and signals when patrol zone 4 received a possible burglary-in-progress call.

> POLICE DISPATCHER: Zone 4.
> ZONE 4: Go ahead.
> DISPATCHER: Zone 4, respond to the alley on the north side Seventh Avenue between Twenty-first and Twenty-second streets. Complainant said she hears banging noise, possible burglary in progress.
> ZONE 4: Ten-four [acknowledgment].
> POLICE DISPATCHER: Zone 3 respond and backup zone 4.
> ZONE 3: Ten-four, coming from Nebraska and Henderson.

[*One minute later*] Zone 4, we're 10-97 [arrived at scene, east end of the alley].

Several minutes later, we advised, "Zone 3, we're 10-97, in the alley west of Twenty-second Street."

Zone 4 yelled, "WE'RE CHASING TWO SUSPECTS RUNNING FROM THE REAR OF HARDWARE STORE WESTBOUND IN THE ALLEY. SHOTS FIRED, SHOTS FIRED."

My partner yelled, "WE'RE TOO CLOSE TO THE BUILDING. I CAN'T GET THE DOOR OPEN!"

I yelled, "BACK UP! BACK UP! GET THE HELL OUT OF THE ALLEY!"

"BULLSHIT!" my partner said.

He pointed his revolver out the car door window and fired off three rounds. The two suspects running toward us stopped and put their hands up. Zone 4 officers slammed them to the ground and handcuffed them.

One of the zone 4 officers, Nick, really was pissed, "Goddamn it! We were right on their asses when you fired at them."

My partner said, "Calm down. I fired into the air."

There was silence. The only sound came from the officers and the suspects, huffing and puffing to catch their breath; and in the distance, many police sirens becoming louder and louder.

"Zone 3 to radio, 10-66 [cancel the responding backup units]. We're 10-15 [prisoners in custody]."

It was 2:00 AM and quiet enough to become sleepy on this cool and breezy early Sunday morning. But now we'd be wide awake until we got off duty. Anyway, with this arrest and shots fired, there was enough paperwork to last until at least 8:00 AM.

Some of the alleyways in Ybor City and in some of the older neighborhoods of Tampa were frequently littered with trash and other junk, rendering them just wide enough to accommodate one vehicle moving in one direction. Some alleys were so narrow that you couldn't open a door wide enough to exit a car unless you stopped adjacent to a doorway where the alley widened.

*

One night, D. J. Halligan was assigned to patrol zone 15 and I was in zone 16. Both zones were geographically located at the southern end of the city in middle-class neighborhoods.

D. J. was working his way south down an alley while I cruised south parallel to him on MacDill Avenue. If a burglar spotted either one of us, he would instinctively flee in the opposite direction, in which case the other would be there to chase him and make an apprehension. Just about halfway down the alley, a burglar ran out a back door.

D. J. yelled, "GOT ONE RUNNING SOUTH! NOW WEST ON EUCLID! ON FOOT, ON FOOT!"

I spotted D. J. running north between houses. I raced around the block just in time to cut the suspect off. When he tried to run around the cruiser, I "tapped" him on the ass with the front bumper, and he slid facedown about twenty feet on a very rough blue pebble roadway. Picking him up and handcuffing him, the multiple abrasions from head to foot were quite noticeable.

The intern at Tampa General Hospital said he'd be one sore bastard for a few days. This guy looked like someone used a sharp grass rake to comb his body then applied a coat of iodine with a four-inch paintbrush. Believe it or not, the doctor released him to us. This poor guy cried all the way to the booking desk.

*

One night, working the downtown zones 1 and 2, a detective unit staking out a building spotted someone in a nearby building and called for backup. My partner, Pete Hopkins,* was driving. We were the first patrol unit on the scene. This was a large two-story commercial building located on Nebraska Avenue. I bailed out and worked my way down a narrow slip between two separate sections of the building. It was so narrow you had to turn sideways to move. Luckily, I was pretty skinny, but anyone larger than average would never have been able to negotiate their way down that slip. The ground was littered with everything from soggy paper to tin cans and mud.

Approaching the end of this slip, I heard someone yell, "He's coming our way!"

In the dark, I could just about make out a human silhouette scurrying up a gutter pipe toward the roof.

Someone yelled, "DETECTIVE, ON THE ROOF! DETECTIVE, ON THE ROOF!" But at first, I could not make out what was being said and instinctively thought an officer may have been in trouble on the roof.

When the subject reached the top of the gutter pipe, I had my .38 Special Smith & Wesson revolver pointed at a human figure. As the upper half of his body was silhouetted against the moonlit sky, I cocked my revolver and almost fired, but didn't.

The suspect was ultimately captured without any violence. He was a fourteen-year-old kid. But at night, without seeing his face, you could believe you were looking at an adult. Over the years, I often wondered how I would have handled the emotional aspect of killing such a young person.

While there was little or no discernible distinction in the law about violent and nonviolent crimes, most officers applied logic and reason when confronted with a shoot or don't-shoot situation. Unfortunately, some officers did not.

*

In 1965, I was training a rookie officer named Don Hand. He had been on the force for less than six months, and though somewhat immature, he displayed above-average ability for patrol work. During the first week of a midnight shift, we apprehended five burglars. This streak began the very first night on patrol. After roll call, we reviewed the previous night's burglaries on the pin map. I was driving and headed straight for a strip of mom and pop stores on Dale Mabry Highway on the west side of town, an area known as Drew Park. Several stores along this strip had been hit the night before.

Turning off my headlights and coasting down behind the stores, Don yelled, "HOLD IT! DON'T MOVE!" We bailed out of the cruiser quickly enough to convince two men, one with a flashlight, the other with a crow bar, that we had them pinned in. Both were barely adults but we soon found out this was not their first burglary. (Catching a burglar on his first crime is rare, like winning the lottery, figuratively speaking of course.)

The next night, we were patrolling the northwest end of zone 12 along West Hillsborough Avenue. We spotted two characters at an all-night Laundromat. These two guys were brothers from Georgia. The older one was twenty-one years old, the younger just eighteen. They claimed to be visiting their mom just across the street in the corner house. The younger kid was cooperative, but the older one was a real wiseass and had a record for burglary.

"No problem, guys," I said. "We'll be seeing you again." But what I was really thinking was *We'll be watching you.*

The very next night after roll call, I drove west on the interstate from the station and then headed north on Armenia Avenue, turning west on the side street just south of the mother's corner house on the next street. I pulled over, turned off the lights and engine, and sat there listening. We could hear movement down the street that sounded like car doors or garage doors opening and closing. Without turning on the headlights, I started up the engine and eased down the street.

As we passed the mother's house on the corner, we could see that the trunk lid of a car parked in the driveway was open. Don hit it with the spotlight, and two human figures ducked—one running toward the house, the other north into an empty lot just east of the house heading toward Hillsborough Avenue.

I called for backup. The suspect who fled was the older brother. When we pulled up, they were loading the car trunk with items stolen from a Sinclair gas station on Hillsborough Avenue, two blocks north of the house. They had tools and oil products, but more interesting was a large heavy brown bag, like the kind used for cement, filled with packs of assorted brands of cigarettes. I had a patrol unit check the Sinclair station, and they confirmed the burglary and the forced opening of the cigarette machine. The younger suspect refused to talk to us; and the mother, of course, was protective of her son.

Thirty minutes later, the older brother was seen ambling across the empty lot toward the house, eating a bag of potato chips. Trying to look surprised, he asked without a hint of nervousness, "What's going on?" He continued to repeat that question with outright indignation after being handcuffed. He said he had just come from the last movie show.

As it turned out, the car was stolen. Their story was that somebody must have pulled into the driveway to load up the stolen property when we pulled up. They stuck to that story. Based on what we had, they were charged with burglary, but we wanted more evidence.

The most common type of physical evidence we search for on a crime scene is latent fingerprints. In this case, we had the crime scene technician, Prewitt,* process the stolen property for fingerprints. Not finding any prints on the tools or oilcans, he began processing the packs of cigarettes. After dusting about half of them, he began to bitch about it. Every so often I would check on Prewitt's progress. Hours later, when we had just about given up hope of getting any fingerprints, Prewitt walked over to us, beaming from ear to ear. We couldn't believe it. He lifted a perfect thumbprint that matched the older brother's prints off the last pack of cigarettes. I'll never forget the brand: Raleigh.

When this case went to court, the suspects pled not guilty. Halfway through the trial, Prewitt showed up ready to testify, holding an eight-by-ten photo of the thumbprint. He was still beaming from ear to ear. I reminded him of all his bitching before he lifted the last print. Later that same day, the suspects finally pled guilty. This was an attempt to make a deal, knowing they were toast with the thumbprint we had.

Fourth night on patrol, still tired from working until 2:00 PM. That same day, we hit the street and within a few minutes received an intrusion (silent) alarm call from the Outpost Lounge on Columbus Drive, just east of Dale Mabry. This was a small lounge and the first building in a string of small businesses extending eastbound.

Following standard procedure, upon arriving at the scene, we positioned our cruiser at one corner of the rear of the building. I advised the dispatcher that we were 10-97 in the rear and that we had a break. I directed backup units to cover the front and east side of the building.

The burglar had popped open a small but accessible bathroom window (the point of entry) at the rear northwest corner of the building. Based on our quick response, we believed he was still in the building. At the northeast (rear) of the building was a screened storage area that also contained a door, allowing access to the interior of the lounge. I told Don to maintain an observation point close to the point of entry, and I assumed a position behind the building to observe the screened area. Within a minute of our arrival, the backup unit arrived in front. Then all hell broke loose.

As the backup unit arrived, the driver, Officer Pete Hopkins,* stopped his cruiser just east of the building, giving him a line of sight north toward the rear and screened area. Although I also had sight of the screened area, Pete observed the suspect break from the area, running to the rear in my direction.

Pete didn't see or know exactly where I was and sped down between the buildings in the cruiser to pursue the suspect. As the suspect came into my view, he spotted me at the same time and turned quickly, running east. I ran in his direction, not knowing Pete was bearing down on him as his cruiser headlights were still off.

Pete yelled into the radio, "GOT ONE RUNNING BEHIND THE BUILDING!" He looked up, saw me crossing in front of his cruiser, applied his brakes—but it was a cold and very wet night. I spotted the cruiser too late and slipped in the wet grass, ending up on the ground facing the cruiser still bearing down on me.

At this point, Pete lost sight of me still sliding fast. I instinctively grabbed the front bumper with both hands, staring straight at the left front tire, which was now only about eighteen inches from my face. The cruiser finally stopped, and I was up and running again. I saw the suspect slip in the grass, and he went down, but he was soon up and running again with me in foot pursuit.

Officer Dick Cloud, also responding to the call, arrived at the east end of the strip; and together we grabbed the suspect.

It was only after the capture, as I returned to the scene with the suspect in hand that I realized that my revolver had slid out of the holster and was gone. These were border patrol holsters, issued by the police department but designed for horseback. It was a very insecure holster for our type of police work. More than once, an officer found himself in a fight when someone came from behind and removed his revolver. Retracing my steps, I luckily found mine.

We had a very busy first week on the midnight shift. We received kudos from the detectives, prosecutor's officer, city council, and the chief for successfully apprehending five burglars in less than a week. It also got me a trip to the University of Georgia for a weeklong burglary workshop, which was a worthwhile trip.

*

Patrol techniques included driving through an area or street, leaving and then doubling back, parking with lights off, hiding and listening. You raced up the street, circling behind buildings as if you knew a burglary was in progress, hoping a burglar would panic and flee a building.

I remember a game plan some officers devised that was dubbed as the Rat Pack. Three or four adjoining patrol units would team up and at random, through our contiguous assigned patrol areas, converge on commercial areas and buildings that were popular repetitive targets for burglars, securing the perimeter of a building and checking all doors, windows and persons or vehicles parked in the area. The results weren't too bad. Burglaries decreased in those areas we attacked, and in some cases, we actually apprehended burglars who were either in the act, getting ready to break in or had just broken in.

*

One night, in zone 4 (Ybor City area), my partner and I responded to an intrusion alarm at a scrap metal junkyard at the east end of Broadway (Seventh Avenue). The building faced Broadway with a six-foot chain-link fence extending from both sides of the building and enclosing the entire complex.

The only public entrance was on the east side of the building outside the fenced area. I parked with my headlights shining toward the fenced-in yard, which covered about an acre of ground.

We waited for our backup unit, and upon their arrival we approached the entrance, noticing the door was ajar and with marks that indicated it had been pried open. Just as we entered, we heard a metallic object hit the floor, and a shadowed figure bolted from the inside toward the loading dock at the rear of the building.

The suspect jumped from the loading dock, fled toward the rear of the yard with my young, inexperienced partner in foot pursuit, yelling, "STOP, OR I'LL SHOOT!"

Now there was no way this guy could have escaped. The fence was topped off with tangled barbed wire, and I was right behind my partner, yelling, "DON'T SHOOT!"

The rookie yelled again, "STOP, OR I'LL SHOOT!"

I yelled again, "NO, NO, GODDAMN IT! DON'T SHOOT!"

From the backup unit outside the fenced area came, "DON'T SHOOT! DON'T SHOOT!"

The suspect then yelled, "DON'T SHOOT! DON'T SHOOT! OH LORD! DON'T SHOOT ME!"

My rookie didn't shoot, and the suspect gave up without any resistance. This guy had been released only one week prior from state prison.

*

One Saturday night while patrolling the northeast section of town, I responded to an intrusion alarm at the Sears & Roebuck department store on Hillsborough Avenue. Security personnel were not on duty after closing. The two-story building covered at least a square block. Without an army of patrol units, there was no way to effectively cover the exterior while the building was searched for suspects. With the exception of one backup unit, all the others in the area were busy on calls. I drove in one direction around the building, checking for a break or suspects, and my backup did likewise in the opposite direction. We met in the rear at the employee's entrance. All the building access points were apparently secure on the exterior, and it would be a thirty- to forty-five minute response time before a Sears security guard arrived to assist in checking the interior. My backup left because he was needed elsewhere.

When the store security guard arrived, we entered the building and began our inspection. Once we reached the second floor, we began our search, moving in opposite directions.

Within one minute, I heard the security guard yelling, "GET YOUR HANDS UP! I'LL SHOOT!"

I ran through the furniture department and saw the security guard pointing his revolver at a subject who was sprawled out on a canopy-covered bed. His hands were covered with a pair of socks, and he was pushing himself with his feet in a futile attempt to move himself backwards, distancing himself from the pointed revolver now only a few feet from his face. The security guard, whose hand was shaking uncontrollably and the gun cocked with his finger on the trigger, was still yelling he would shoot the suspect.

The security guard was a man in his fifties and obviously incapable of maintaining self-control. With his finger on the trigger and his hand shaking so violently, I thought for sure he would shoot the suspect. If he fired at such a close range, the shot was almost certain to be fatal. In an attempt to distract his attention from the suspect, I eased up to the security guard and leaned forward in his line of vision so he could see my face. The suspect now was frantic, believing he was going to be shot, and there wasn't anything he could do to prevent it.

I quietly directed the guard to point his revolver toward the floor, reset the hammer, and holster it. I was reasonably convinced the suspect was not armed, and in any case, I was in an excellent position to stop him if he tried anything. The guard holstered his revolver, and I handcuffed the suspect. The look on the suspect's face told me he was very happy to see me. He had just been released from prison and hitched a ride to Tampa, entered the store, and remained there, concealing himself at closing time.

Once he was sure everyone was gone, he covered his hands with a pair of socks to prevent leaving any fingerprints. He rifled through several cash registers and set off the (silent) intrusion alarm upon entering the cafeteria adjacent to the furniture department. He hadn't eaten all day and decided to grab a bite while he was there. He was probably eating while I was waiting for the guard to arrive to check the building. After eating, he became tired and promptly fell asleep on the bed.

When the guard confronted the suspect with his revolver, three people were terrified—the guard was frightened of the suspect, the suspect was scared because he thought surely he would die that night, and I was extremely alarmed because I was sure this man was going to be killed in an unjustified shooting. After the incident was over, I charged the suspect with burglary with intent to commit larceny.

When the dust settled, Sergeant Haze* a large cigar-smoking man, arrived on the scene. The sergeant had a distrust of any officer he did not like, especially any officer who would challenge him even for a legitimate reason. He told me I didn't have a good burglary case against the suspect because we found him sleeping, and there was no evidence to prove he intended to steal anything. He discounted my evidence of the suspect wearing a pair of socks on his hands, saying maybe his hands were cold—in July?

The suspect, however, had already been charged and booked. The sergeant did not appreciate it when I informed him months later that the suspect was convicted of burglary. This particular sergeant was one to hold grudges.

*

Observing a small window at the point of entry of a burglary would lead most people to think *juvenile*. Not always so. Cruising down an alley in Sulfur Springs one midnight shift, my partner and I happened upon an open window. A single room air conditioner occupied the bottom half of the window, and the top half had been sealed with a piece of plywood which had been pulled out and placed on top of the roof just above the air conditioner. We called for a unit to cover the front. We were familiar with this particular strip of mom and pop stores—all were a single room, some with a bathroom installed against the rear interior wall. This business was a beauty salon with such a bathroom.

When our backup unit advised they had arrived and had the front door covered, my partner, older and senior to me, merely said, "Well, Joe, I'm the same height as you, but—"

I said, "Yeah, I know. Get my skinny ass through the window because your ass is wider than mine!" So I did.

I managed to wiggle through the opening but not without having to remove my gun belt; my partner handed my sidearm back to me when I got inside. The backup unit covered me from their front door position. Observing the interior through the front window, they indicated no movement or anything appearing to be disturbed inside. However, the bathroom door was ajar; so once upright inside, I edged, revolver in hand, along the sidewall of the bathroom.

If the burglar was still in the store, he had to be in the bathroom. I decided it was safer to search the bathroom than to expose myself by working my way to the front door, letting the other officers in. As I rounded the front corner of the bathroom, I peered through the open space behind the partially open door and spotted a hefty-sized pair of engineer boots. Poking my gun barrel along the opening of the door, flashlight above the revolver, I spotted the suspect behind the door, pressed and frozen against the wall.

I asked him if he could see my gun, and a quivering voice responded, "Oh, yeah."

I said, "Don't move."

He said, "Oh, don't worry, Officer, I won't."

Once I could see his hands, he was ordered to lie on the floor facedown. With the bathroom door now wide open, I unlocked the front door, keeping an eye on my catch. Once we stood him up, he had to be about six foot three inches and not at all skinny.

I asked, "How the hell did you get through that window?"

His response: "It wasn't easy."

*

The humorous details about this next incident circulated through most roll calls for several days, causing much uncontrollable laughter. In the early morning hours after the bars closed, a burglar finished his last drink, left a bar, and went back behind the building into the alley. He was searching for a way to access the common roof of the stores that stretched for a block on Nebraska Avenue.

His target was the mom and pop grocery store on the corner.

The burglar located a trap door on the roof, pried it open, and entered into the crawl space between the main roof and the suspended ceiling. This guy was still somewhat intoxicated but was able to negotiate his way along the crawl space toward the end of the building where the grocery store was located.

Unbeknownst to the burglar, Ed, the owner, had arrived at 5:00 AM as he does every day in order to prepare for opening at 6:00 AM. The burglar was also unaware that the first thing Ed did was to brew a pot of coffee, knowing the two-man patrol unit working the area routinely stopped by the store. They enjoyed an early morning cup of coffee with him before the store actually opened for business.

While the burglar worked his way closer, Ed was behind the counter, the officers were leaning on the customer's side, all three with cups of coffee in hand carrying on a conversation. Mr. Burglar by this time was tired and hung over, perspiring in his haste to make his entry quickly and quietly. The guy then lost his balance and came crashing down through the suspended ceiling panels, landing on the floor between the two officers who instinctively and simultaneously drew their revolvers, pointing them directly at the burglar without uttering a word.

The burglar looked at the officers, realizing that two guns were trained mere inches from his face and said, "OH SHIT! Don't . . . don't shoot. I'm not violent!"

Both officers holstered their weapons and grabbed the burglar by the arms, but they laughed so hard they were momentarily unable to handcuff him.

When the news media called the shift commander later that morning for information and asked for the suspect's name, the captain replied, "Mr. Dumb Loser." This was the kind of morning when both the midnight shift officers and the oncoming day shift officers spent a good fifteen to twenty minutes in laughing mode—very therapeutic in law enforcement.

*

The humor on the job never ends. It can't. If it did, we wouldn't survive the frustration of dealing with the lowest human element and their violence, depravity, and viciousness. There are numerous incidents in police work that are nothing short of hilarious. Humor helps police officers endure and cope with the worst the job brings.

*

The Sulfur Springs beat was located at the northern end, about a mile or two from the city limits and was populated by mostly native Floridians, affectionately called "crackers." However, some very tough characters frequented the local bars. Anytime you were walking that beat and came upon a sleeping drunk in an alley, you made sure you had a backup and the paddy wagon on scene before waking him.

One night while walking an alley, I happened upon a guy passed out against the rear door of a closed bar. I called for the wagon. Zone 10, the Sulfur Springs patrol unit, came by when they heard my radio transmission. When the wagon arrived, we got this guy up on his feet and just about dragged him to the rear of the wagon.

Suddenly, he came alive. This guy was well over six feet tall with arms the size of a professional wrestler's, fully tattooed with hearts, the Confederate stars and bars flag, and even a clichéd Mom. A true blue cracker. D. J. Halligan, not a small guy himself, had one arm—and I thought I had the other. We were trying to keep him from raising his arms above his waistline, but they kept coming up no matter how hard we held him.

He opened his eyes, never turning his head, glanced sideways at D. J. then at me, and spoke in a soft, deep voice. "If you let my arms go, I'll get in the wagon."

There was no need for him to say it twice. We complied as if a marine drill sergeant had just given us orders.

*

Officer Ralph Poundhand,* was a big-boned Georgian cracker who never punched anyone. All he had to do was slam you on the side of your head with his opened ten-pound banana-finger hands, and down you'd go. Ralph walked a beat like no one I ever knew in this business. He was about six foot two, and for every step he took, a shorter man had to keep up with him by taking three steps. The guy never stood still. I think he caught more burglars than any other cop who ever walked a beat.

One night while Ralph was walking the beat, he happened upon a burglary in progress at the Sulfur Springs Tap Bar on Nebraska Avenue, the main thoroughfare of Sulfur Springs. Other bars and an array of local mom and pop stores lined Nebraska Avenue. It was about 4:00 AM. The bars were closed, and Ralph was flicking his flashlight as he approached and passed the stores along the street.

When he got to the Sulfur Springs Tap, he shined his light through the plate glass window, spotting two guys behind the bar. One was crouched down with his hands in the cash register, no more than ten feet from Ralph, separated only by the window. The second suspect stood at the far end of the bar.

Ralph drew his service revolver, pointed it at the closest suspect, and yelled, "Freeze! Get your hands up!"

The guy closest to Ralph stood with his hands up at the same time the guy in the rear squatted down and began to scurry away. Ralph fired one round through the plate glass window, and the guy closest to him screamed then ran so fast to the rear that he actually ran over his partner in crime as they both headed for the back door.

Ralph ran around to the rear and chased one of the suspects down the alley. He knew he couldn't run fast enough to catch him and tried to shoot him in the ass, but his gun misfired.

D. J. and I were assigned to zone 10 that night and responded to the scene. The owner was notified and arrived about fifteen minutes later.

Seeing a perfectly round hole just the size of a bullet from Ralph's .38 caliber revolver in the center of his large plate glass window, the owner came unglued. From the bullet hole, cracks ran in every direction to the extreme ends of the glass. It looked like a road map.

The owner, knowing Ralph, jumped up and down, yelling, "Ralph, you dumb bastard. I had ten bucks in the cash register, but it will cost me at least two hundred to replace the window."

D. J. and I had to turn and walk away because we couldn't stop laughing. On its way, the bullet also hit a row of large pickle jars on the bar, splattering pickles and pickle juice all over the furniture, then traveled through a window at the far end of the bar, which was the burglars' point of entry, finally hit the windshield of a neighbor's Lincoln Continental parked in a yard across the alleyway.

Meanwhile, because Ralph's gun misfired the second time he pulled the trigger, the burglars managed to get away. So much for

Ralph's nighttime walking beat assignment. The sergeant put him back on the paddy wagon assignment.

The irony of all this is that most officers do not like a walking beat. Those that do, of course, usually get their wish. In Ralph's case, he liked the walking beat, but the department just could not "afford" it!

5

Close Encounters of a Dangerous Kind

In police work, black holes have nothing to do with the universe. They are things that cops trip over or into when chasing bad guys in the dark.

Starting out as a rookie in a patrol car with a senior officer puts you in a frame of mind that if you are not like this old timer, if your philosophical views of people and police work are different than his, then you are not going to make it through probation.

Uppermost in a seasoned officer's mind are a rookie's physical, mental, and emotional abilities. If there are two traits that are critical for becoming a professional police officer, they are truthfulness and courage. Every individual possesses varying personality traits, some weaker, some stronger. But only a highly ethical person with dauntless courage can survive in this business and be recognized as a true professional. And yet, a small percentage of undesirables still manage to slip through and accumulate years of tenure.

I can recall officers backed into a locker room corner by fellow officers and being physically threatened when they had failed to back up a fellow officer because they were scared. Most at that point knew their days were numbered and eventually resigned. Others were fired.

One such individual on my squad was a man I'll refer to as Yellow Rabbit*. It became obvious that on potentially dangerous calls he would hold back and make sure at least one other officer was on the scene before he was. This was the case, whether or not he was responding to his own call or he was assigned as a backup unit.

Yellow Rabbit was in his first year on the job and still on probation. One night, I received a call to back up Yellow Rabbit on a suspicious person/car called in by a waitress at a drive-in ice cream stand. Yellow Rabbit was only a few blocks away while I had to respond from about three miles out. The police dispatcher provided a detailed description of both the suspects and the car, yet when I arrived, the suspects were gone. Yellow Rabbit actually pulled up after I did.

Approaching the waitress, I could see she was angry. She pointed at Yellow Rabbit and said, "What the hell is wrong with him? Is he a coward?" The waitress went on to say that the suspect was parked at the edge of the drive-in property when, and she pointed to Yellow Rabbit again, *that officer*, drove up, looked at the suspicious car, and then just drove off.

I asked Yellow Rabbit to explain to me why he failed to approach the suspect's car or at least contain the situation until I arrived. He mumbled something I couldn't hear and drove off. I apologized to the waitress, but it was an embarrassing situation.

Several other officers and I decided it was time to speak to the sergeant about Yellow Rabbit. Our sergeant was a good person, intelligent, and we were told, a decorated World War II veteran. But he was also lazy. Unless we specifically called on him for guidance, the majority of his energy was utilized for picking up reports.

We expressed our anger and demanded Yellow Rabbit be fired. The sergeant made excuses but did not pursue our demand. Believe it or not, Yellow Rabbit was not fired. He continued to shirk his duty to back up other officers but fortunately, his lengthy tenure with the department was something of a rarity.

Generally, officers such as Yellow Rabbit were suspect all along, but it generally took an incident when such individuals were faced with a dangerous situation and backed down, froze, or merely disappeared in the melee that the truth about them was finally made public. Even though these men, in the end, proved their own cowardice, it's important that no one be branded a coward before or unless there's irrefutable evidence to confirm it.

*

I recall one supervisor with a reputation for being a tough guy. He had the physical size to make one believe he could handle himself well. But size alone is worthless if you lack the intestinal fortitude to put it in gear. This supervisor, the ranking man on the scene, when shots were fired at police officers, failed to take command of the situation. I had my suspicions about his lack of courage all along but lacking real evidence, to this day I have not revealed my feelings about him.

In the initial stages of a crisis, it may take a moment or two to filter through what has happened before getting your ass in gear and taking command. But failure to take control could result in absolute disaster.

There is nothing wrong with having a healthy dose of fear. We all experience it and fear can keep you on your toes, alerting you to real danger. But if you want to be a police officer, you better learn to overcome the desire to disengage when the shit hits the fan and the lives of your fellow officers and innocent citizens are on the line. That's what the badge, oath, honor, and commitment are all about.

However, I have never agreed with the philosophy that an officer is a coward merely because he employs the option of resolving problems by means other than force. I've seen officers kick ass when the adversary was at a disadvantage, whether because of the psychological impact of the police uniform and gun or because the subject was just too drunk or stoned to engage in a fight. Beating somebody's ass with a stick doesn't take courage.

At times, moral certitude ensures success in resolving human conflict, for example, avoiding the need to engage in a physical altercation. The ability to take control of a volatile situation includes being patient. Dealing with an angry person requires knowing how to talk someone down off an emotionally charged plateau and sometimes, displaying compassion can go a long way in avoiding a physical confrontation.

Police use of force should always be the last resort in the resolution of problems, both legally and ethically. But when an officer is faced with an immediate life-threatening situation, with little wiggle room, chances are, "Now, now, sir. Please calm down," ain't gonna cut it.

A good example, as the patrol division commander, I reviewed a report that described two patrol officers happening on an incident at night in the middle of a busy four-lane road. They observed a man beating somebody with a baseball bat. Both officers bailed out of the cruiser and challenged the assailant with a polite order to please drop the bat.

The suspect then turned his attention from the injured victim on the ground to the officers. Several times the officers requested he drop the bat, but suddenly, the two police officers had become targets of the suspect, who still clearly wasn't thinking about dropping the bat. He didn't seem at all interested in complying with clear-cut orders.

Finally, one of the officers yelled, "Drop the fucking bat, or we'll blow your goddamn brains out!"

Guess what? The guy immediately dropped the bat. End of story.

The most dangerous aspect of policing the streets is complacency, falling into a routine, and bringing your personal problems to the job. Stopping so many traffic violators day in and day out without any negative consequences, reinforces bad habits, which can lead an officer down that dangerous alley of death in disguise. I constantly counseled young officers about the importance of carrying themselves in a manner exuding confidence. They must be approachable, yet their body language must signal those who might contemplate doing serious harm, "I'm on to you, buddy, so watch your step!"

I recall incidents of officers handling situations that turned violent, and they were within inches and seconds from death. Sometimes they survived, but too often, they didn't.

On July 24, 1981, just before leaving my office, I ran into Vice Detective Gerald Rauft who was assigned to the tactical division. At the time, I was commander of the detective division.

Knowing the vice team was going out on a drug deal, I told Rauft, "Be careful."

He responded, "Okay, Major Joe."

I then called my wife, Alice, and asked what refreshments she wanted me to bring home as friends were coming over to play cards. While on the phone with Alice, I detected something was wrong.

When I asked, she just said, "Oh, I don't know, but I have a strange feeling that something bad is going to happen."

I said, "Okay, honey, I'll be home in a few minutes."

I arrived home less than twenty minutes later, and Alice met me at the door, acting jittery.

I asked, "Now, what's this feeling you have?"

She said, "I've had this feeling a number of times in my life and something bad always happens."

At that moment, the phone rang. Detective Rauft had been shot and killed in the drug bust. He was trying to rescue Detective Bob Ulricksen who was wounded and being held hostage by a drug dealer. The drug dealer barricaded himself in a bedroom. Rauft tried to force the bedroom door open with his shoulder but was killed when the drug dealer fired a shot through the door. The bullet pierced the door, entered Rauft's upper arm then into his heart.

Sergeant Pete Ambraz was one of the first officers to respond, forced the bedroom door open and the suspect was apprehended.

In 1975, we lost three officers in as many months:

> September 27—Detective Ken Berlin was killed in a traffic crash.
> October 23—Sergeant Richard "Dick" Cloud was shot and killed by a hit man when answering his front door. Dick was working with federal agents in an organized crime investigation.
> November 3—Officer Anthony "Tony" Williams was shot and killed when, while off duty, he walked into an armed robbery in progress at a convenience store.

On November 4, 1983, Sergeant Gary Pricher was killed by a drunk driver when he stepped out of a police vehicle to help children wandering around outside of a broken-down school bus on the interstate highway. I was told his last words were, "You kids get back off the roadway before you get run over."

Other Tampa police officers who were killed in the line of duty between December 1988 and 2001: Officer Porfirio Soto, Officer Norris Epps, Detectives Randy Bell and Ricky Childers, and Officer Lois Marrero.

*

Extensive studies reveal officers in potentially dangerous situations, such as traffic stops, are unknowingly being sized up.

The studies reveal that a number of these officers are often killed with their own guns. Because the officer is taken by surprise, he or she often fails to react and take control of the situation. In a matter of seconds, the officer is shot and the suspect flees.

Patrolling alone one night, I pulled a car over, emerging from an alley without headlights on. Before pulling over the driver, I informed the police dispatcher of my approximate location, the tag number and description of the car, and the number of occupants. Once the car was stopped, I stepped out of the cruiser, my gun holster unsnapped, and stood behind the car door for cover. In this particular case, the driver was out of the car in seconds, walking back toward me. I could see his hands, studied his face and gave him orders to stop in front of the cruiser and place both hands on the hood. Then two other males exited the car, and I ordered them back inside. They ignored me and continued to approach the cruiser.

The radio microphone was hanging over the car door. I depressed the transmission button. "Zone 12, send backup. Although I officially called for backup, on the night shift, it's traditional for the adjacent patrol zone car, if available, to drive by your location as a safety measure.

By this time, my firearm was up and pointed at my deaf friends. I said, "Okay, guys, which one of you bastards do I kill first? The one who takes another step closer? The one who reaches into his pocket? I'm close enough to drop the two of you within as many seconds. Now, let's try this again. I want you facedown on the ground or for sure, each one of you will at the very least end up with a bullet smashing into your kneecap. You have no idea how painful that is. If you don't think I'll shoot, just keep coming. I'm tired and in no mood for your bullshit and not too sure I can control myself with this gun before my backup gets here."

The driver froze in front of the cruiser, and his two deaf friends went facedown on the pavement—no more misunderstandings.

*

Sometimes you dive into a situation without giving any consideration to caution. Perhaps it could be the flight of a traffic violator you just stopped. Instinctively, you take off after him without any thought of the suspect turning, producing a handgun, and shooting at you. All you have on your mind is that he's getting away, and you have to catch him. In most cases, an experienced officer will proceed with some mental preparation, anticipating and visualizing the suspect turning on him. This mental thought process, to some degree, prepares the officer to react more quickly than simply focusing on catching the suspect.

*

One night, I responded to a burglary complaint in a black neighborhood. I met the complainant, an elderly black lady, distraught over someone breaking into her meager little wood-framed home and stealing what little bit of cash she had saved. She worked twelve hours a day as a maid and had very little to show for her hard years of work.

The odds of apprehending the suspect and recovering the victim's money in these cases are slim to none. Eventually, burglars get caught, but by that time all money has been spent and valuables have long been sold.

While I took the report, trying to console the lady as much as I could, a car with no lights on kept roaring by the house, speeding first up the street and then back down. After six or seven passes with my marked cruiser parked in front of the house, I realized this clown was speeding back and forth, saying, "Ha! What you gonna do, cop? You can't catch me."

Once I gathered all the information, I waited until Flash Gordon passed again, and I hustled to my cruiser. I slid down low in the driver's seat, started the engine, but kept all lights off. When Flash drove by again, I took off after him without turning on any lights. When I got right up on his ass, I hit the siren, flipped on the overhead lights, and the chase was on.

He made several turns and headed east on Osborne Avenue toward Fortieth Street. I kept the dispatcher informed of my direction of travel and speed. Flash slowed down as he approached Fortieth Street, turned into a used car lot, and bailed out of the car while it was still moving.

I told the dispatcher, "ON FOOT! Fortieth and Osborne." As I bailed out of the cruiser, I slammed the gearshift up toward the park position.

The suspect was a black male, running west on a residential side street. I was gaining on him as we ran through front yards. I heard the sirens of responding backup units, but I had no radio contact as portables were not available at that time. Catching up to Flash, I lunged, grabbing him by the belt. He swung around, knocked me down, and I landed face up in an old bathtub half full of rainwater. I quickly got back in the race and finally tackled the guy.

I heard the backup units close by, racing up and down the streets trying to find me. Porch lights started coming on. A black lady standing in her doorway wanted to know what was happening. I identified myself as a police officer and asked her to call the police. The lights then went out, and I heard doors shutting. I finally managed to handcuff the suspect.

While walking him back to the parking lot, Officer Frank Broce spotted me and rendered assistance. I explained to Frank what happened when I bailed out of my cruiser and chased down the suspect.

Frank looked skeptical and said, "Joe, I knew you were very fast but not that fast."

It seems that my cruiser had popped into reverse instead of park, rolled back out of the car lot and traveled about one-half of a block north of where I bailed out. It stopped when the rear wheels rolled into a rut on the shoulder of the road.

When questioned, the suspect admitted he took the car from the used car lot, believing if he got it back before the police caught him, he wouldn't be arrested for auto theft. The interesting thing was that during the entire foot chase of the suspect, I never gave any thought that he might be armed. Luckily for me, he wasn't.

*

I clearly remember my first felony arrest. I was just out of the police academy a few weeks and working the evening shift. My partner, Pete Hopkins, and I received information at roll call about an auto thief who had just been released from prison—his fetish was stealing 1957 Chevys. His last arrest, the one that sent him to state prison, was for stealing a 1957 Chevy. It was the Christmas season, and we were working the downtown area.

We were headed north on Florida Avenue when Pete spotted a 1957 red and white Chevy on the H&R used car lot. Remembering the roll call information, he slowed down and alerted me. At the same time, the Chevy began moving in reverse, and the headlights came on momentarily. We both saw a man bolt from the driver's side of the Chevy, which had rolled forward into its original parking space.

Pete slammed on the brakes, and I jumped out in foot pursuit toward the rear of the car lot and east to Marion Street. I lost sight of the suspect when he turned north in front of a two-story house on Marion. Within seconds, I rounded the corner, but he was nowhere in sight. I looked into the foyer of the house, but it was too dark to see anything. When I bailed out of the patrol car, being the rookie that I was, I didn't grab my flashlight.

I then turned my attention to the street, looking north, when I heard a voice yell out, "State Beverage agents. Come out of there, and put your hands up now."

I looked behind me and saw an agent in a kneeling position pointing a sawed-off shotgun toward the foyer of the house. The suspect stepped out onto the sidewalk from the foyer with his hands down at his side and his head down as if to say, "You got me."

Before I could get my rookie ass in gear, two Florida State Beverage agents were on this guy like a bass on a bug. They then turned to me and introduced themselves. They were on a stakeout when they observed the suspect run from the Chevy with me in foot pursuit. They couldn't challenge the suspect because I was too close behind him and would have been in the line of fire.

One agent said, "You're obviously a rookie or you would have had your sidearm out of the holster when you rounded the corner looking for the suspect."

He was right. A more experienced officer would have approached the corner cautiously, prepared to shoot if necessary. It's far better to lose a suspect than walk into an ambush. Again, a lesson learned about approaching with caution to avoid walking into a deadly encounter. The danger of this job is not that every criminal you encounter is armed and prepared to kill you—it's just the opposite. You will encounter a far greater number of subjects who are either wanted or are committing a crime that will not resort to deadly force against an officer; it's that one in a hundred suspects that's armed and will not hesitate to kill you that turns out to be the deadly problem.

There are instances you just don't have time to size up a situation, only react to it, so always anticipate a violent encounter.

*

I was assigned to the communications section for about three months after suffering a knee injury. Even after returning to full patrol duty, I kept my right knee wrapped in an Ace bandage. What luck! The first day back on the street and the knee was put to the test. I was patrolling on the day shift when the dispatcher broadcast the description of an escaped prisoner in the area. I circled the block, heading toward the last location he had been seen.

I turned down a side street and spotted a white male walking toward me about two blocks away. He was walking fast, turning and looking back, then he spotted my cruiser and immediately changed direction, running between two houses, and I momentarily lost sight of him. I advised the dispatcher that I was in foot pursuit headed north between the houses in the 700 block of Genesee. I spotted the suspect again, running in a field behind the row of houses. I could feel a slight twinge in my knee as I ran. Unwittingly, the suspect was about to pass in front of me but couldn't see me because of a row of hedges separating us.

I ran toward the hedge, timing his arrival and planned to run between the hedges, covering my face with my arms. But as I got closer, I could see a wire fence woven along the hedges. I had to stop short or jump over the three-foot fence. I thought briefly about my knee giving out and then jumped, and, wouldn't you know it, I cleared the fence, coming down first on my injured knee. I landed, took about three steps and was right on the suspect. Taking him to the ground, I realized he was armed with a knife. I grabbed for the knife, pinning his arm down, then I jammed two fingers up his nose with the palm of my right hand under and against his chin, forcing his head up, cramming both fingers as deeply as I could in his nostrils. (Not very nice, but extremely effective). Now his concerns were pain and breathing, not the knife. He wisely decided to cooperate.

*

At another time, I was riding solo in patrol zone 10 in Sulfur Springs. It was a busy Friday night, mostly dealing with drunk drivers and disturbance calls. I was assigned a call to a local bar, the Dew Drop Inn. I was close and started rolling in that direction, while the dispatcher provided me with descriptive information.

The dispatcher said, "Man being held at gunpoint at the bar. The unidentified complainant stated the suspect is a white male, forty- to forty-five years old, about 200 pounds, with thick gray hair. He's wearing a black and red plaid long-sleeved shirt and Levi's." The dispatcher finished with "Use caution. No backup available. The paddy wagon is just leaving the booking desk and is headed your way."

I couldn't wait for backup because someone could have been killed before my backup could arrive.

I stepped up to the front entrance of the tavern. It was like a saloon out of the Wild West. It had been raining, and the ground around the sidewalk was muddy. Country western music was playing, and it was crowded inside. Entering, I scoped out the bar area. If I ever found out who called this in, I'd kiss them. The detailed description lit up the suspect like a blinking neon sign, saying, "Here I am."

I headed toward the bar and patrons started moving out of my path. I was keyed up, anticipating this guy was going to spot me before

I could get to him. I was a good target, with no immediate cover if he decided to panic at the sight of the police uniform and began to shoot. If I walked too fast he would surely spot me, but getting within range quickly to grab his gun was critical. The suspect and his potential victim were seated on swiveling bar stools.

The suspect had a menacing look on his face as he appeared to be threatening and pressing a handgun against the victim's midsection. The suspect's back was partially toward me. The victim spotted me and was trying not to alert the suspect, but his eyes widened even more when he realized I was headed his way. There were people at the bar and seated at tables close by, but they were clueless about what was happening. Other patrons, though, were tracking my movement toward the bar. If shooting erupted, others were also at high risk of ending up as victims. Moving closer, I observed that the suspect was so angry and engrossed in menacing the victim he had no idea what was coming. He was turned to his right, so I approached him on his left or blind side.

Now I was within reach, standing inches from him, and he still didn't see me. He was holding the gun in his right hand. I couldn't hear everything he was saying above the music, but he was obviously very angry. I tapped him on the left shoulder. He turned away from the victim, away from his gun hand. He looked up in surprise and froze long enough for me to reach around and grab the cylinder of his revolver, gripping it very tightly, rendering him unable to pull the trigger.

Then all hell broke loose. He couldn't shoot the gun, but he refused to let go of it. I wheeled him around, throwing him from the swivel stool, but he hung on to the gun. Patrons were flying out the door, windows, diving behind the bar, under tables, and just about anywhere they felt their asses would not be exposed.

Now this guy was really pissed off. I had a good grip on the gun, but "Billy the Kid" was determined to regain control of it. I had to maintain control of his gun and hope he didn't think about taking mine. We struggled while heading out the door where there was more room. We wrestled over the gun and ended up on the walkway and then down we went in the muddy gutter.

While I was still trying to wrench the gun from his grip, Officer Franz Warner arrived, jumped out of the paddy wagon, and together, we finally secured "Billy the Kid."

Once he was placed in the wagon, I retrieved the gun for evidence. Still a bit winded, I propped one foot up on the bottom step of the wagon while talking to Franz. I was complaining about my brand-new uniform shoes getting muddy and scratched from grappling with "Billy the Kid," but now he was in the wagon, yelling he had to take a piss.

I said, "Well, go ahead and piss then."

My foot was still propped up on the step and the wagon was parked on an incline. Suddenly, the urine ran down and out the rear door of the wagon onto my shoe and foot. He was pissing, and now I was pissed.

In most of these cases, you have to put a positive spin on the end results with no one dead or seriously injured, just pissed off—and in this case, I was also pissed on. Oh well, it's funny now, years after the fact.

*

I remember another wrestling match with a skid row character described to me by older officers when I was still considered a rookie. At roll call the sergeant assigned me to walk the skid row beat. On the way out the back door, some of my mates smiled and said to say hello to Stumpy.

I asked, "Who's Stumpy?"

An officer yelled back at me as he climbed into his cruiser, "You'll find out when you have to arrest him."

Well, I did meet Stumpy. Not that night but later that week. On Friday night, while passing the Saratoga Bar, I heard glasses breaking and profanity spewing. Obviously, a fight was brewing or was actually in progress. I worked my way toward the back of the bar to break it up. I grabbed the aggressor who wasn't very big, about one hundred twenty pounds. His opponent's face was a bloody mess, one eye swollen shut and the other going that way. As we exited the bar, my friend began struggling to break free. I grabbed his shoulder to spin him around. When he tried to sucker punch me, I rocked back and grabbed him by the wrist, but he pulled away. I grabbed him by the wrist again, and he pulled free again. Finally, I realized he had no hand. There'd be no handcuffing this guy.

I had to throw him down and just sit on the little twerp until the paddy wagon arrived. I told Stumpy the other officers said to say hello. He told me what I could go do to myself.

*

Officer CM* was overheard by other patrol units advising the dispatcher he was going 10-50 (stopping a vehicle) on a suspected drunk driver. The backup unit arrived to observe Officer CM standing by the open driver's door of his cruiser and demanding the suspect, a large black male, place his hands on his head. The suspect started walking toward CM who pulled his revolver out quickly, bringing it up, intending to point it at the suspect.

But CM was so nervous the forward motion caused him to fling his gun out of his own hand, and it landed in a mud puddle at the feet of the suspect. CM froze. The suspect stopped, looked down, slowly bent over, picked up the gun by the barrel, attempted to wipe the gun clean, and handed it back to CM. He then turned and leaned against the cruiser, fully cooperative and, in fact, was very respectful and even nonchalant.

The backup officer re-holstered his revolver and walked over to CM and said, "CM, when you draw your gun, HOLD ON TO IT! Okay?"

*

In another incident, a special crime enforcement unit was staking out a number of convenience stores throughout the city. The unit was comprised of about four squads of officers, a sergeant in charge of each, and commanded by one captain and a lieutenant. Based on robbery statistics, the most vulnerable stores were selected for the stakeout assignments. Two or three undercover cars, each with two plainclothes officers, patrolled a select area, covering two to four or five convenience stores. Each store selected for this operation had a camera and audio setup, which is monitored at a fixed command post.

When a robbery profile was evident, the monitoring officer alerted the cover cars in that area, and they responded to the crime scene. In the majority of cases, units waited until the robber exited the store to reduce the risk of innocent people, including the store clerk, being hurt.

In one case, one of the officers assigned observed a robbery going on, and it appeared the clerk might be in danger. The officer decided it was too risky to wait for backup and entered the store, drawing his sidearm, which was secured in a belt-clip holster. The officer challenged the suspect with his gun pointed directly at him. But he didn't realize that when he drew his gun it was still in the holster, which had unhinged itself from the belt. The suspect stood there with a surprised look on his face, but he was not willing to take on the police. At the same time, several officers entered the store to assist.

When the suspect was secured, the officer trying to reholster his gun realized that all the time he was covering the suspect, his snub-nosed revolver was still stuck in the holster. It was a good laugh at roll calls for the next few days.

I could just imagine the headlines if the officer had been forced to fire at the suspect—"Robbery suspect shot by police officer, but chokes to death on gun holster."

*

One night when I was a patrol captain (shift commander), my lieutenant expressed concern that two convenience stores had been robbed twice, each in a period of two weeks. The investigation revealed the same robber was alternating his two targets every few days. We gauged the time elements and the probability of when the next robbery was going to happen. We decided to stake out both stores, which were only blocks apart.

The best strategy was to conceal an officer with a shotgun in the storeroom. The clerks in both stores would recognize the robber and were coached to alert the officer when and if the suspect returned. I directed the lieutenant to select two seasoned officers, one for each store, and two chase cars to respond in the event of a robbery. The lieutenant selected one corporal, JA*, to cover one of the stores.

Within a few minutes on the first night of the stakeout, the store clerk blurted out, "Oh shit! Here he comes!" When JA heard the robbery suspect demand money, he charged out of the storeroom, pointing the shotgun, and screaming at the suspect to get on the floor.

JA was nervous times ten and instead of just sliding one shotgun round into the gun chamber so it could be fired, for every step he took toward the suspect he jacked a shotgun round out of the chamber, emptying the shotgun. When the chase cars (backup) arrived on the scene, they found that JA had the suspect on the floor with the barrel of the shotgun jammed against his mouth, and shotgun rounds scattered around on the floor. The sound and sight of the shotgun convinced the suspect to just lie there frozen.

In a post incident interview, the store clerk said that when the corporal charged out of the supply room, waving the shotgun and screaming so loudly the clerk couldn't understand a word the officer said, his first reaction was to dive behind the robber for protection.

In the robbery suspect's post incident interview, he said he was convinced he was a dead man. There was plenty of roll call conversation about that one.

6

Police Use of Force

Use of force is use of violence. Violence begets violence. Violence is a tool police use to enforce the law and in defense of themselves, their fellow police officers and innocent citizens. Police using violence is fighting fire with fire.

On average each year, more than 50,000 police officers are assaulted, injured, and disabled. And a police officer is killed in the line of duty every day and a half.

Police officers confronted with subjects of superior physical strength and agility had one advantage. Most individuals recognized the officer's authority (the uniform, badge, gun, arrest powers, etc.,) and also the officer's option to employ the use of deadly force if a fight was not going his or her way. Therefore, in most confrontations, officers needed only to exercise verbal commands or minimal use of force.

The standard for exercising police authority and make an arrest begins with verbal persuasion, escalating to necessary levels of physical force and if the encounter becomes potentially deadly for the officer, the use of deadly force is justified.

*

One evening, an energetic young officer followed up on roll call information about a John Smith,* wanted on a felony—bad checks charge. When Energetic Earl knocked on Smith's front door, Smith bolted out the back door with the officer in foot pursuit down an alley.

He couldn't catch the suspect; so he pulled his gun, took aim, and fired. Fortunately, he missed. The officer then called for his sergeant.

When the sergeant arrived, he was furious. "What the hell is wrong with you?" he yelled.

After a few minutes of ranting and raving, I whispered to the sergeant, "*We are drawing a crowd here in the alley.*"

In the meantime, a white male, very upset, stepped out from behind a garbage can in the alley, approached us, offered his hands, and surrendered.

This is one example where an officer failed to use good judgment. Though the law back then technically justified the use of deadly force to capture a fleeing felon, philosophically and morally it was considered wrong unless the suspect was perceived as dangerous.

*

One night at roll call, when I was a patrol officer, the sergeant handed Officer Poundhand and me a misdemeanor warrant to serve on a white male, Brent Watson,* who was wanted for battery. The sergeant told us that the battery victim, a white male, Tom Bailey,* called from the Robles Park Bar and said the subject, Watson, was currently at the bar. The tavern was about five or ten minutes from the police station and was on the edge of the Robles Park housing project. Not too many weekends passed without a fight or two at this tavern.

As we entered the bar, we noticed the victim was sitting with three other men at a table. He looked at us, didn't say a word, and just pointed out Watson sitting at the bar. We approached the bar and advised Watson he was under arrest. He acknowledged the warrant, looked over at Bailey, and started out the door with us.

That was our mistake. As we approached the front entrance, Watson ran past us and commenced to pound the hell out of Bailey. We grabbed Watson, trying to handcuff him as we should have done to begin with.

All hell broke loose. It seems half the bar patrons were friends of Bailey's and the other half were Watson fans. I grabbed Watson around the neck from behind, trying to work my way out the door. Poundhand, as I have said, was a big man and just having a ball slamming anyone within range upside the head with his catcher's mitt-sized opened hands.

Acknowledging that Ralph was holding his own, I dragged Watson outside so I could handcuff him and load him into the cruiser. Watson's brother decided to introduce himself to me by grabbing me around the neck from behind, but I had a good hold of Watson with one arm around his neck.

By this time, the paddy wagon had arrived, along with two or three other patrol units. We started loading up the wagon, including Watson and his brother. Bailey stood on the sidewalk, laughing and cussing at Watson as he was being placed in the wagon.

Officer B. J. Anderson, not knowing the warrant situation, reached over, grabbed Bailey, and said, "Okay, loudmouth, we'll give you a free ride to the booking desk too."

The last thing I saw was Watson sitting just inside the wagon with a grin on his face and Bailey trying to backpedal out of the wagon doorway, yelling, "No, no, oh, no!"

Just as the door of the wagon closed, I saw that Watson had Bailey by the shirt collar. We could hear him yelling help, which he repeated several times as the wagon drove off.

*

One night, we received a domestic dispute call in the Robles Park housing project. I was training a new officer, Jim Whitley. Jim was a Vietnam vet and had experienced some pretty tough combat up close. He was quiet and seemed laid back. It took me by surprise the first time I observed him become angry.

We had stopped a man who matched the general description of a wanted suspect. When we encountered the man on foot, he became indignant and uttered some disparaging remarks about the police. Jim came unglued. I had to grab him and push him away when he advanced on the man with what was an obvious intent to administer his version of appropriate discipline. I later counseled Jim, and I am glad to say I had no other problems of that nature with him.

Anyhow, when we arrived at Robles Park, we didn't have an accurate apartment address and had to make inquiries of several residents. We were directed to a location across a courtyard. While en route, we observed a very large white female—not obese, just big—outside an apartment, leaning against the building assisted by another woman. As we got closer, we could see her bloodied head and clothes. Her head was down when we approached and identified ourselves. When she looked up, both eyes were swollen shut. The best way I can describe them is that they looked like there were two golf balls under her eyelids, and they were sewn shut. She had been beaten badly on the face. Her nose was smashed flat against her face, and her head bore four or five large knots that were lacerated and bleeding. Some teeth were knocked out, and her mouth and lips were cut and swollen so badly she could hardly talk.

Apparently, her live-in boyfriend, a longshoreman, came home drunk and angry and beat her because dinner wasn't ready. I suddenly had a great desire to put him in an institution that always served meals on time: prison.

I could see Jim was doing all he could to control himself. His jaws were tight, and his head was down, looking at the ground. We began our search of the apartment. When we reached the bathroom, the door was locked from the inside. I told the guy inside to come out, that we knew he was there and would kick in the door. He came out fighting. Jim and I were not in a very good frame of mind after seeing what he had done to his girlfriend. We fought this guy over the staircase, through the living room, and out the door. He landed several blows on both Jim and me. He was tough, hard, and fast, but we beat him until he finally ended up on the ground handcuffed. He had to be treated at the hospital.

It would be a lie to say that both Jim and I weren't angry or that we didn't intend to inflict any punishment on this tough guy. In fact, I guess it's okay now to reveal that when he came out of the bathroom fighting, my silent thoughts were *Yes, there is a god.*

*

One evening shift, while riding solo in the Ybor City area, I heard zone 1 dispatched to a loud drunk at the rear door of a tavern on Seventh Avenue (Broadway). I was close by, and it was a slow night, so I headed that way.

When I arrived, a black male was standing on the back steps, waving his arms, and cussing at the wind. He had been ejected from the tavern and was not a happy camper. As I approached, he continued yelling obscenities but made no threatening moves toward me. When I tried to talk and humor him, he wasn't quick to respond or cooperate. He rambled on without any concern about my presence.

Within a minute, zone 1 Officer Ed Collins* and his partner approached the scene. Collins was from the old school and had no tolerance for drunks, especially black drunks. This drunk was running his mouth, and Collins brought out his nightstick, fully intending to pound our drunken friend on the head until he was horizontal.

I had heard stories of Collins really doing serious damage to people, especially black men. He had no intention of allowing me or his partner to interfere with his wrath, but I had no intention of standing by while he assaulted this guy. I stepped in front of the drunk and faced off with Collins.

He approached me, yelling, "Get the hell out of my way."

I responded, "Collins, nobody's hurting this man. He's my prisoner now."

Collins answered, "It's my fucking call, now move."

I told Collins's partner to radio our sergeant to respond to the scene and told Collins, "I was here first, he's my prisoner, put your nightstick away because you're not beating this man." He began yelling and cussing while I stood fast. He never got an opportunity to hurt the drunk.

I had heard that when Collins was patrolling one night, he stepped out of the cruiser to confront a black male who was apparently just talking loudly. When the black man didn't remove his hat in a display of respect for the police as Collins approached, he hit him on the head several times with his nightstick.

I had no desire to mistreat anyone. Anger was common in this line of work, and you had to learn to control your emotions—not always an easy thing to do.

*

The old city stockade housed inmates found guilty of minor offenses against the city: drunkenness, disturbance, petty theft, trespassing, vagrancy, profanity, and a host of other violations short of serious crimes. It was not a pleasant place to hang your hat. The stockade facility itself was dirty and dingy, and there was always a dank odor lingering throughout the inmate areas.

Security was less than adequate. Jail guards were not really trained to do the job of controlling restive inmates. Except for the cellblock sections, an inmate could just about walk off the premises from anywhere, anytime.

Many of the guards were not young men and so, were incapable of grappling with inmates who were hardworking individuals with physical strength beyond the average man. They were city garbage men, construction workers, etc., with jobs requiring a significant level of muscle development for hard labor. They were also men raised hard with not much education, and fighting was their method of choice for resolving any disagreements. Many were also alcoholics.

Inmates who demonstrated they could behave had the opportunity to work off their sentences. For instance, a man with a ninety-day sentence could work one day and erase three days off his sentence. Depending upon their reliability, inmates could even end up driving city vehicles to repair shops and back to city departments. Others worked off their time on the back of a garbage truck. Some had special skills, as noted elsewhere in this book.

The police were routinely summoned to the city stockade to handle uncontrollable inmates. One night, my partner, Reid Keldy, and I responded to the stockade chow hall. An inmate refused to return to his cell. He had shoved several guards and helped himself to more food.

The guard who escorted us to the chow hall was of average size and I'd guess fifty- to fifty-five years old. When he entered the chow hall, the inmate glanced over, saw us, but never reacted. He just sat there drinking his coffee and smoking a cigarette. He was big, well over six feet and over two hundred pounds.

The guard tried once more to convince the inmate to return to his cell. We stood back but were close enough to step in if need be. The guard said, "Okay, Tom*, it's time to get back to your cell now. These officers don't want to take you back to jail and charge you with resisting. All that's going to do is add more time to your sentence. So what do you say? You want to go back to your cell now?"

The inmate, not a bit rattled by our presence, said, "I'm not going back to that m—f—ing nasty dark cell. I don't care about the fucking cops. They don't scare me. I just want to be left alone now. You hear?"

When the guard tried to grab him by the arm, the inmate shoved him back, then stood up, and turned his attention to us, both arms pressed against his sides with clenched fists and a tight jaw. His frown and the look in his eyes said, "If you cops want me, here I am."

Reid and I walked right up to him, and I said, "Come on, guy. This ain't good for any of us. How about just going back to your cell?"

Before I could say anything more, he grabbed Reid by the belt, swung him, then raised him up, and slammed him to the floor. I heard a cracking sound when Reid's lower back hit the cement.

Reid was now momentarily out of it. I swung out, striking the inmate on the jaw with my fist. I gave it all I had, but all it did was to rock the inmate back one step. He stopped and shook his head, and I thought, *Oh, shit.*

Reid was still on the floor in obvious pain, and the guard was standing by the exit door ready to run.

Before the inmate could reset, I swung around behind him and simultaneously brought my left arm around his neck and was able to pull him back, rendering him off balance. I braced myself with my right leg back, left leg forward and slightly bent, clasping my left hand and right hands together, pulling back against the inmate's throat with the front of my head against the back of his. Now he couldn't pull forward because I had him off balance, backwards, and locked in. My left wrist was pressing against his windpipe, which I pulled back and sideways, effectively cutting off his airflow. All he cared about was getting air, but within seconds, he was out of it.

By this time, Reid was back on his feet and we quickly handcuffed the inmate. He regained consciousness within a few seconds but had no fight left in him.

That neck restraint called *hadaka-jime* (Japanese pronunciation: hadakajima) saved my ass many, many times. It was part of my training in the service while on a military judo team.

*

I received a call in reference to a man beating his girlfriend. When I arrived, there were two females, the mother and her adult daughter, standing in the open doorway, waiting for the police. The younger woman was crying, and as I reached the front door, I realized she was pregnant. Her dress was torn around the collar and down her back to about the waist. The suspect, her boyfriend, had left with another male when the mother called the police. The younger woman had a swollen left eye, her mouth was lacerated along the lower lip, and she bore fresh red bruises around her neck.

She was a pretty and petite girl. She described the boyfriend, one Roger Morrison.* My interview revealed to me she was a good person because though she was in pain, she only concerned herself with the welfare of the coming child.

Armed with descriptions of Morrison and his buddy, Bill Butthead,* the car they were driving and their hangouts, I was highly motivated to catch this guy. I began looking for the car at local neighborhood bars. Failing to locate them after about a forty-five-minute search, I pulled into a shopping center parking lot. I parked, facing the street Morrison would have to take if he decided to return and get his girlfriend.

I began writing the battery report, looking up frequently to check the street. Bingo. I spotted the car cutting across the parking lot. Morrison and Butthead spotted me at the same time. At first, it appeared they were going to flee but thought better of it and stopped.

I ordered the driver to get out of the car and place his hands on the roof. I knew by the description it was Butthead, a real wiseass. I looked over at the passenger, and I knew it was that brave soul who had beaten the hell out of his pregnant girlfriend.

"What the fuck are you stopping us for?" were Butthead's first words.

I responded, "Only one of us will be asking questions, and it won't be you or your real tough friend."

Butthead had been drinking but was steady on his feet. When I began to frisk him for weapons, he turned, and I pushed him back against the car. He had a lit cigarette in his hand, which I didn't see because I was trying to keep my eyes on both subjects at the same time.

When my face was less than two feet from him, he said, "Keep your goddamn hands off me, pig," and flipped the cigarette, which bounced off the left side of my forehead. It hadn't burned me, but I immediately reacted by punching him on the right side of his jaw, discouraging any other macho-man displays.

By this time, my backup had arrived, and Morrison decided to depart on foot. I chased him for about a hundred feet, grabbing him by his belt. I spun him around and ran him back toward the police cruiser, and all the time he was calling me every kind of a son of a bitch that he could think of. He continued to struggle, and when we reached the back of the cruiser, I forced him facedown on the trunk lid. He became silent. Both were charged with resisting arrest, and Morrison was charged with battery on his girlfriend.

Several weeks later, another officer asked me, "Hey, Joe, do you know a guy named Morrison?"

I answered, "Yeah, I do. Why?"

"Well, he came up to me last night at the A&W Root Beer stand and said that when he finds you, he's going to kick your ass."

I can't count the number of times someone I arrested threatened to come back and kick my ass once they were out of jail.

Over the next month or so, a number of my colleagues told me they had also run into Morrison and that he was looking for me. One midnight shift, I was cruising south on Dale Mabry and spotted Morrison's car parked at Frisch's Big Boy restaurant. Showdown time.

I pulled into the parking lot, drove by the front entrance, and spotted him sitting up at the counter with his back to the door. I parked, walked in, and approached him while he was running his bigmouth. I sat down alongside of him, and he still didn't see me because he was turned away, preoccupied with trying to impress someone else. However, he finally turned to look at me when I tapped him on the shoulder.

I said, "I understand you've been looking for me to beat my ass?"

He sat frozen with his mouth agape, and I then said, "Well, damn it, you can't beat my ass if you are sitting on yours, so get up on your feet."

He froze, turned red, and began sweating—and I just walked away. No more feedback about kicking my ass.

7

Deadly Force Encounters

*The saying "You can never be too careful" can be echoed
incessantly in our profession and where there are those humorous
incidents in police work, within seconds tragedy awaits.*

Decades ago, state laws on police use of force were loosely translated to include the use of deadly force to apprehend fleeing felony suspects, making no clear distinction between violent and nonviolent crimes.

One case that stands out in my mind occurred on the day shift in Ybor City. An officer received and responded to a residential burglary-in-progress call. Within seconds of advising the police dispatcher that he had arrived on the scene, he was back on the radio, advising that he had shot the burglar and needed paramedics. I was the on-duty field lieutenant and responded to the scene.

The suspect, a black male in his late teens, entered the house when nobody was home. When I arrived, the suspect was lying facedown in the alley located behind the house. He was shot once in the back and had died at the scene. Soon after my arrival, two assistants from the prosecutor's office arrived to initiate their investigation.

All such deaths are investigated by the state attorney's office, and it was clear from the start that they would justify this shooting. The officer stated that he notified the police dispatcher when he arrived at the scene. As he walked toward the rear of the house, he heard footsteps from inside headed in the same direction. He ran to the rear and observed a young black male exit the rear door, jump off the porch, and run toward the alleyway.

The officer yelled, "Stop, or I'll shoot."

Ignoring the warning, the suspect scaled a waist-high cement wall that bordered the alley and homes along that street. As the suspect entered the alley, the officer, without attempting to scale the cement wall and pursue the suspect on foot, fired one shot, striking the suspect in the back; he then fell to the ground.

The officer, a young man, was in reasonably good shape and might have used other means of apprehending the suspect. Though the shooting was declared justified, I knew I would not have employed deadly force to apprehend a suspect for this type of crime.

*

On August 3, 1976, at 3:47 AM, Corporal Bentley Thomas responded to a shooting at the Old Orleans Motel on Dale Mabry Highway. Bentley was not assigned to this call but was very close when it was assigned to another patrol unit.

Bentley arrived at 3:51 AM and advised the dispatcher he was on scene. It was too dark to see, but upon hearing someone plead, "Please don't shoot," Bentley, placing himself in danger, approached the front entrance, attempting to draw the attention of the suspect away from the intended victim. He challenged the suspect to drop his weapon, which turned out to be an automatic rifle. Bentley was shot several times in the leg and knee. Returning fire, he then took cover behind his cruiser while approximately twenty more rounds were fired at him.

Bentley remained composed and alerted police communications that he was shot, relaying information about the suspect. The end result was a murder victim, one dead suspect, and another arrested. Bentley's actions were, without a doubt, courageous.

*

Patrolling West Tampa on the midnight shift, November 15, 1971, Officer Joe Walker spotted a car fitting the description of one involved in a robbery and radioed the police dispatcher that he was going to initiate a stop. The description was unique: a red or maroon Lincoln with discoloration around the wheel wells.

How could you miss it? Joe took what he thought were reasonable safety precautions when he pulled the car over. The driver was well dressed and cooperative. Joe had no visible violations but stalled the driver, until his backup could arrive, to determine if he could glean sufficient information to hold the guy.

The dispatcher called Joe's radio number; and in that split second when he turned to pick up the microphone, the suspect pulled a handgun and fired several rounds, striking Joe in the head and neck. He fell across the front seat of the cruiser and though fully conscious, realized he was paralyzed. He could not move at all. He felt and saw the suspect leaning over him, apparently looking for something. The suspect pushed Joe out onto the ground, frantically searching for his driver's license.

In the meantime, Joe could feel he was regaining his mobility and removed his sidearm from its holster. The suspect turned and fired another shot at Joe, grazing his right arm. Joe returned fire, striking the suspect, who then fled across Dale Mabry Highway. Joe fired his last shot, fatally hitting the suspect.

How many times has a news article described a police officer killing a suspect when a family member of the deceased asked the question, "Why couldn't the cop just shoot him in the leg? Why did he have to shoot to kill him?" Officer Joe Walker's experience should answer that question. The suspect, though shot, managed to flee before being shot again—this time fatally.

Joe Walker will tell you he watched the suspect very closely and was taken by surprise when he was shot because there was no perception of danger in his initial contact with the suspect. All the time the suspect was just waiting for that right moment, that split second Joe turned away. That's all it took. Joe went on to achieve the rank of captain, a well-deserved achievement for a dedicated and brave officer.

*

In 1956 Officer Lamarcus Larry, one of the few black Tampa police officers, while working an off duty job in the area of North Boulevard and Main Street in West Tampa, encountered an individual shooting up a bar.

After a brief foot chase the suspect took refuge in an apartment building. Lamarcus kicked in the door. He spotted the suspect's silhouette on the staircase wall and realized he was reloading his handgun. The suspect fired twice striking Lamarcus in the chest and the liver. Returning fire, Lamarcus killed the suspect. Lamarcus recovered from his wounds and returned to full duty.

Not only did he serve more than twenty years with the police department before retiring, he also served his country as a reservist in the United States Air Force for more than twenty years—retiring after achieving the rank of Chief Master Sergeant.

You know his wife Bobby and his family must be very proud.

*

In another case, vice detectives were working the Central Avenue district, just east of the downtown Tampa area. Sergeant Lee Vodin, while seated in his unmarked unit, was approached by a well-known black pimp. The sergeant, who was very familiar with this individual, suspected the worst and was prepared when the pimp opened fire but missed his target. The sergeant didn't. The pimp ran toward Central Avenue with the sergeant in foot pursuit. The suspect turned and fired at the sergeant as he ran. Several blocks into the chase, the pimp dropped dead.

Even though the sergeant's .38 caliber round struck the pimp in the heart, he was still able to run several more blocks and return fire before he died.

*

A Tampa public school intrusion alarm was activated, and police communications dispatched patrol units to the school. The first unit on the scene confirmed the intrusion was a burglary. En route, another officer, Sergeant Bob Pennington, spotted a car in the area of the burglary with no headlights on. He stopped the vehicle and approached it on foot.

The driver exited the vehicle and confronted the officer, who ordered him to show his hands. The subject reached into his pocket, producing what appeared to be a chrome pistol. The subject failed to obey the officer's command to drop it, so the officer shot and wounded the suspect. It turned out the subject, a supermarket employee, had a handheld chromed metal device used for stamping prices on food products. At night, with limited lighting, the object could reasonably be mistaken for a handgun.

The state attorney's office justified the officer's actions for several reasons: the officer was responding to a burglary-in-progress call, the subject was driving in the immediate area of the school without his headlights on, and then produced what could have been mistaken for a gun, ignoring the officer's command to drop it. Although it was not a firearm, the officer had reason to believe his life might have been in jeopardy because the subject was acting suspiciously and appeared to have a handgun.

The state attorney's findings in this case are supported by a recent appellate court ruling: "The Fourth Circuit Court of Appeals [*Anderson v. Russell*], found reasonable an officer, [in this case, Russell] using deadly force against an unarmed man [Anderson] who the officer believed was reaching for a weapon.

*

One Christmas eve, in the mid-1960s, a veteran officer and his rookie partner stopped a plumbing company pickup truck on the north end of Tampa. The truck was traveling with no headlights on. It was a very cold night. When the driver could not dispel the officers' suspicion, he was placed in the rear seat of the police cruiser. The officers failed to thoroughly search and handcuff the suspect because it was cold, and they were in a hurry to get back into the cruiser. At that point, the suspect pulled a small caliber pistol and fired shots, striking both officers.

While the senior officer recovered from his wounds, the rookie's wound resulted in permanent paralysis. This shooting resulted in probationary police officers receiving full disability benefits from the Tampa Firefighters and Police Officers' Pension Fund. Up until that time, officers and firemen could not receive full benefits until they had completed six months of service.

*

An officer working in an off-duty capacity for a supermarket arrested an adult male for shoplifting a carton of cigarettes. While waiting out front for a patrol car, the suspect grabbed the officer's holstered gun; and in the ensuing struggle, the officer was shot five times. Miraculously, he survived. Also shot was the off-duty Temple Terrace police chief, who witnessed the struggle and shooting. When he attempted to assist the wounded officer, he took one in the face but also survived. A manhunt resulted in the capture of the suspect in a rural area of a neighboring county.

The shoplifter, knowing he was headed back to prison because he was on parole, wanted to disarm the officer because he feared being shot while fleeing. He said after being captured he did not intend to shoot the officer.

In both the above cases, the suspects should have been immediately handcuffed. In that window of the first few minutes of an encounter with a suspect, the officer has the advantage because his or her attention, in most cases, is focused on the suspect. Once that window is closed, the suspect, if not restrained, begins thinking and decides going to prison is not in his plans for the future and attempts to flee or take the officer down.

*

At roll call one midnight shift, the sergeant read off information about one of our local thugs, Ralph Slug.* The detectives believed he was involved in a number of burglaries on the west side of town.

I checked Slug's usual hangouts, then I spotted his car leaving a bar heading south of Dale Mabry Highway. Before making my stop, I advised the dispatcher to alert the adjoining patrol units of my general location. I made the stop and scanned the interior of Slug's car, noting a front seat passenger. Slug stepped out of his car just as I stepped out of the cruiser. As he approached me, he was ordered to place both hands flat on the hood. Slug was being unusually courteous. Although this was my first encounter with him, I knew his demeanor was a farce.

After some standard questions, he was released, but I didn't for a minute think burglary was his main or only illegal activity. Call it what you want. A *gut feeling* is the most common vernacular.

I think what I suspected most was his outward effort to be as polite as he could. But he never looked directly at me when he talked. His eyes kept sliding from one side to the other. I sensed that this guy's brain was swirling as if he was trying to determine if he should attack me and, if so, how he should do it. I gave him no opening and no room. His politeness only heightened my suspicion that his behavior was intended to be a diversionary tactic in hopes that I would let my guard down. But I didn't.

Several years later, officers responded to a suspicious-person call at a west side restaurant. When they walked in on a robbery-in-progress, a gun battle ensued. No officers were hurt, but one robber was killed—Ralph Slug.

*

In the 1960s, it was common practice for officers to initiate police action in any potentially dangerous situation without waiting for a backup unit. If you happened upon a possible burglary, you would call for another patrol unit but had the option to enter the building and conduct a solo search. This was not always a good idea.

Traffic Officer William Krikava was assigned to the Traffic Division's Enforcement Unit. This unit consisted of several squads of motorcycle officers who patrolled the city to issue traffic citations to violators. They became involved in patrol work only when patrol officers were busy and not available to answer calls or respond as a backup unit.

Just past midnight on January 1, 1965, Krikava was patrolling on his motorcycle in the area of South Dale Mabry when a patrol unit was assigned to a possible burglary in progress at a dress shop in the middle of a shopping strip. Krikava, just several blocks from the scene, responded. He pulled around the rear of the building and worked his way north, checking for some sign of which rear door in the line of stores was the dress shop. He looked for evidence of a forced entry into a store, or at least an address or business name.

As a rule, patrol units on the approach to a burglar (intrusion) alarm or actual burglary-in-progress call will be as quiet as possible, turning off their headlights, then their engine, coasting to a stop in a strategic location on the perimeter of the target building. Every little noise intensifies a burglar's already heightened senses. He's already keyed up, adrenaline flowing, and every noise or movement that would under normal circumstances be overlooked is picked up.

Once he located the dress shop, Krikava entered alone through the rear door. In the next few seconds, the burglar opened fire as he ran past Krikava, who was now blocking his escape route. Krikava, though shot and going down, managed to fire several shots, striking the suspect as he fled out the rear door.

Upon their arrival, the patrol units found a dying Krikava, called for an ambulance, and searched for the suspect. When located, he too was wounded.

A little later, the police dispatcher advised the officers on the scene that Krikava had died. Meanwhile, the ambulance transporting the burglary suspect sped to the hospital at a brisk five miles per hour.

At the time this happened, a group of officers—including me—were celebrating the New Year with our wives at Fort Homer Hesterly. A uniformed officer working the dance off duty came over and advised us about Krikava being shot and killed. That ended the celebration. Not exactly the way we wanted the New Year to begin. But this wasn't the first time that a celebration was interrupted because an officer was shot, wounded, seriously injured, or killed, nor unfortunately would it be the last.

*

I recall several shootings with unintentional targets. Causes ranged from anger to a high-stress situation and horseplay.

The first police shooting in Tampa that I can recall resulting in a lawsuit involved a vehicle pursuit of a traffic violator. The patrol officer notified the police dispatcher that he was in pursuit of a motorcycle. After several minutes, the violator, a black male, decided to stop and pulled off into a parking lot in the area of Dale Mabry Highway and Bay-to-Bay Boulevard. The officer was so angry and emotionally charged he pulled out his sidearm, a .38 caliber revolver, and approached the violator who was still sitting on his motorcycle. The officer grabbed the violator by the shirt collar, yelling at him, waving the gun in his face. The violator used his arm in an attempt to redirect the gun from being pointed at him, resulting in the gun discharging and the bullet striking the violator in the head, killing him. The officer not only lost his job, he was charged with manslaughter. I believe it was this shooting that prompted our police chief and the Hillsborough county sheriff to coordinate the drafting of a police use of deadly force policy.

*

In another shooting incident, an officer and a jail guard, both working for the Tampa Police Department, had been neighbors and friends since childhood. One day, the officer entered the locker room and started clowning around with his jailer friend. Somehow, while the officer poked the jailer in fun with his nightstick, the jailer grabbed it. The officer, in jest, pulled out his .38 caliber revolver, pointed it at his friend who jerked at the nightstick—the gun fired, striking the jailer in the heart. It was fatal.

The officer lost his job, was criminally charged and you can only imagine how this preventable tragedy changed his life and the lives of his family and his friend's family. Because these men were acting like boys, friendly horseplay turned to tragedy.

The third incident involved a civil deputy who was serving legal papers on an individual within the city limits of Tampa. When the subject became aggressive, the deputy called for assistance. When several Tampa police officers arrived, the subject opened fire on all of them. A gun battle ensued and the armed civil deputy, unbeknownst to the police officers, concealed himself in the bushes nearby. His movement aroused the suspicion of the officers, shots were exchanged, and the civil deputy was shot by the officers. Fortunately, he survived.

Patrol officers must always be alert by being aware of their immediate surroundings, maintaining a safe distance between themselves and adversaries, and keeping in mind that police officers are killed in a multitude of encounters that they themselves allow to inevitably become "routine." The horseplay, described above, is an example of officers themselves becoming careless in the routine handling of firearms. A good analogy is that many people first learning to drive a car are extremely cautious, but once driving becomes a "routine" activity for them, they become careless, even reckless.

Tampa Police Tactical Response Team (TRT)
Circa—early 1980(s)

Old Orleans shooting, Aug. 3, 1976

8

To Chase or Not to Chase

You can stop hundreds of cars for traffic violations, write a ticket or give a warning, and be on your way. Then you attempt to stop a violator whose driver's license has been suspended. Spotting those overhead red and blue lights flashing, with images of jail time, violators often panic and choose the gas pedal over the brake pedal.

In most cases, they end up being caught anyway, and their problems are tenfold with the judge. Then there are those individuals who, because of their chosen professions (burglars, robbers, rapists, thieves, etc.,) cannot cooperate with a police officer's demand to pull over, so the chase is on.

High-speed chases are emotionally charged events, probably second only to a shoot-out or related deadly force encounters.

One night, I pulled over a teenager for speeding. While writing the ticket, I heard tires squealing two blocks north of my location on Florida Avenue, which runs one way north. When I looked up, a car was barreling toward me, driving the wrong way with no headlights on. I tried to wave the driver over to no avail, so I jumped back to avoid being struck, and he continued south on Florida Avenue. An unmarked vice unit was in pursuit and when passing me, he yelled, "Get on him."

I threw my ticket book to the kid I had stopped and said, "Wait here." I then jumped into my cruiser and headed south on Florida

Avenue. Generally, a marked patrol unit is the lead unit in a chase. I was attempting to take the lead in the pursuit, but the vice unit refused to relinquish the primary pursuit position and remained directly behind the fleeing suspect. Fortunately, it was a late weekday night with very little traffic on the road. I clocked the pursuing vice unit at ninety miles per hour.

The suspect turned west on Zack Street, then back northbound on Tampa Street, which is one-way south. Still traveling at high speed, he approached the front of the police building at Tampa Street and Henderson Avenue with both the vice unit and me close behind.

The midnight shift's roll call was over and officers were preparing to go on patrol when they heard the chase. They scrambled to the front of the police building on Tampa Street and tried to set up a roadblock, but our speedy friend wove his way through the makeshift roadblock and continued north. Approaching Columbus Drive, approximately four blocks north of the police station, he slammed into a telephone pole. I saw the sparks flying as he made contact.

As quickly as I stopped and got out of my cruiser, the very angry vice detective was on this guy like a cat on a crippled mouse. The suspect was trapped behind the steering wheel of the car. When he crashed into the pole, he received significant injuries to his face. I managed to pull the vice detective away from the suspect but not before he fully expressed himself with both large hands in the shape of fists.

Before I returned to the spot where I had stopped the teenager, I was convinced that with so much time having elapsed, he must have thrown the ticket book on the ground and driven off; but to my surprise, he was still where I had left him, awaiting my return. I voided the ticket and sent him on his way with a stern warning.

High-speed chases are inherently very dangerous. We could argue that the chase should have been abandoned by the police, though there was little criticism by police management for conducting the chase. Pursuits, in fact, were a long accepted practice.

*

Patrolling the north end one evening shift while it was still daylight, I walked up to the takeout window at the White Tower burger restaurant, ordered a cup of coffee, and returned to my cruiser. Hearing tires squealing just north of my location on Florida Avenue, I observed a car traveling at a high rate of speed.

Taking chase, I overtook the car, pulled it over, and asked the driver, who looked to be in his late teens, for his driver's license.

I recognized his name immediately. He was the teenage son of one of our patrol captains. He was polite and respectful, but I felt there was no way I could justify only a verbal warning. His driving was reckless, and I issued him a traffic citation.

Later that night, entering the locker room at shift change, the word already had reached the oncoming shift. Walking to my locker, I passed several officers. It was obvious they knew what I had done. While changing my clothes, someone several rows over asked in a loud voice, "I wonder who the son of a bitch was who gave our captain's son a reckless driving ticket?"

There was dead silence and several pairs of eyes turned to me. Approaching Officer Loudmouth, I said, "I'm the son of a bitch who wrote that ticket on that reckless driver who could have killed someone the way he was driving, even someone like maybe your son, wife, or mom." Loudmouth said nothing more, nor did anyone else.

Several days later, I received a message to report to the captain's office. He wanted to hear directly from me just what his son had done. I explained it, emphasizing his son's respectful demeanor. The captain thanked me for writing the citation, adding, "He's a good kid but is still growing up. What you did will help him get there." Whew.

I issued my share of verbal warnings but at some point, lines must be drawn. To say I never gave a friend or another cop a break would be a lie. You can't be in this business and not step over the line occasionally. I'm not talking about criminality or corruption, just traffic violations and other minor infractions. Cops are imperfect and are still recruited from the human race.

*

In another incident, I was criticized by my peers for abandoning a chase. While on patrol in the afternoon, about the time children were coming home from school, I observed a motorcycle pass me going in the opposite direction on Armenia Avenue, just south of Buffalo Avenue. He spotted my cruiser and changed lanes to increase his distance from me. I turned around and caught up to him at the traffic light.

When he turned east on Buffalo Avenue, I flipped on the overhead lights, and the chase was on. He proceeded east then south along the Hillsborough River into a residential neighborhood. As I continued the pursuit, we entered an area full of schoolchildren, and I advised police communications of my decision to abandon the chase.

That evening in the locker room, a number of my fellow officers criticized and ridiculed me for abandoning the chase.

My response was "It wasn't your decision to make. It was mine, and I really don't give a shit whether you agree with it or not. There were schoolchildren in the area. How many of you have kids who walk home from school? Are you all telling me you wouldn't have a problem with an officer coming to your front door to tell you your ten-year-old son or daughter was killed because the police were chasing a teenager on a motorcycle? AM I to believe your response would be 'Well, that's okay, you had to chase the guy.'" I heard not a peep from any of them.

Prior to leaving the station that evening, I was called into the office. The teenager I was chasing was brought to the police station by his father to turn him in. He thanked me for considering the safety of not only his son but of the others in the neighborhood. The kid fled because he didn't have a driver's license.

My decision to take enforcement action carried the same intent: prevent death and serious injury. Issuing this young boy a citation would hopefully prevent a repeat violation in the future. Abandoning the motorcycle chase prevented the potential for serious injury or worse, a death.

*

Patrolling along Waters Avenue checking buildings one midnight shift, I observed a Corvette traveling westbound run the red light at Armenia Avenue. My cruiser was a Plymouth Fury. When I caught up with the Corvette, I flipped on my overhead lights; and the driver decided to lose me, and off he went.

As I was heading out into the county, the police dispatcher notified the sheriff's office about my chase. The fleeing driver turned north on Dale Mabry Highway. There was virtually no traffic on the road. Several miles north of Waters Avenue, Dale Mabry was totally undeveloped. The highway was bordered on both sides by swamp and forest.

Within moments, I spotted a deputy in a patrol cruiser off to my right on the shoulder of the road. He fell in behind me. We didn't have direct radio contact and could only communicate through our respective dispatchers. I had the Corvette clocked at over one hundred miles per hour, and I was what we referred to as "flat out," which means the gas pedal is on the floor and the speedometer indicator is out of sight. The deputy, who was driving a brand-new pursuit model cruiser, wanted to take the primary lead position. I agreed, knowing his cruiser was better suited for the primary position. I slowed down below one hundred miles per hour and let the deputy pass me.

What happened next took place in a matter of seconds at a very high speed. The deputy passed me in the southbound lane, pulling up parallel to the Corvette. The Corvette appeared to be slowing down, but then he abruptly swerved in front of the deputy, causing him to slam on his brakes, unaware that another deputy I observed through my peripheral vision with no headlights on was in the process of passing me. When the first deputy slammed on his brakes, it caused the deputy alongside of me to panic and slam on his brakes, causing him to spin out of control right in my path of travel. I stayed off my brakes so I wouldn't spin out of control, but all I could do was keep turning to the right away from the deputy. While he ended up on the shoulder of the road, I managed to get back up onto the roadway and back in the chase.

I spotted the Corvette stopped and the marked sheriff's unit behind him. I came to a stop. When I approached on foot, the deputy was standing about ten feet back from the driver, who was leaning on his Corvette with his arms folded. I reached for my handcuffs and for one brief moment I thought (as the suspect apparently also thought by my facial expression) that he was going to get his ass beaten. However, I managed to stay cool and after blurting out a few expletives, I handcuffed the suspect. In the meantime, our spinning deputy managed to get back on the road and finally caught up with us.

He came out of his cruiser, nightstick in hand, heading for the suspect, who by this time had realized he was in the company of three pissed-off police officers on a lonely, deserted road. The other deputy and I had to grab the angry deputy and keep him from pulverizing our prisoner, who by now was in tears.

His was one of the original model Corvettes, but the suspect had just rebuilt the engine; the only reason we caught him was that the engine had become too hot and seized up.

Once our friend was secured in the paddy wagon, the deputy in the marked cruiser turned to me and said, "Do you know how fast you were going?"

I said, "Well, according to my speedometer, one hundred twenty miles per hour. I assume that's how fast I was going."

He responded, "I had you clocked at one hundred and thirty-five miles per hour."

On the way back to town I was still keyed up and was traveling at about thirty-five miles per hour when my right front tire blew out. I can only imagine a blowout at one hundred and thirty-five miles per hour. If the tire had blown out during the chase, I doubt that I would have survived. They could've picked up my body parts with an ink blotter and a pair of tweezers.

*

On a day shift patrolling the Ybor City area, my partner and I were attempting to stop a car for a red light violation when the violator decided he'd rather not get involved and sped off. My partner was driving. We lost sight of the violator briefly when he turned north onto a street, which is uphill at that point. When we turned north, my partner abruptly slammed on the brakes. Our elusive friend had driven for about a half block north of Broadway, bailed out of the car, and fled on foot but took the time to shift the car into neutral, causing it to roll back down the hill.

Talk about an accident waiting to happen! I believe our patrol car was a 1963 Dodge Dart. But whatever model it was, it had the push-button drive feature in lieu of the traditional gearshift. My partner desperately tried to punch "R" to back up. I think he punched every button and, in fact, managed to punch the reverse button, but he was hitting them so fast he punched right out of reverse just about the time the rear end of the suspect's car slammed into us. We shared one word simultaneously—"Shit!" Oh, and yes, it was a stolen car.

*

When you spend a third of your life driving a patrol car, many, many things happen to you on the road, much more so than to the average driver. One midnight shift, riding solo in the Sulfur Springs area, I was working my way westbound on the north side of Waters Avenue, checking storefronts. When a pickup truck traveling eastbound passed me, I noted it had no headlights on. The driver then turned south onto a side street.

While still driving west, I managed to look back over my shoulder, trying to keep the truck in sight. I decided to make a U-turn and catch up with No Lights Larry. Waters Avenue wasn't very wide and coming out of my U-turn. I came to an abrupt stop with the passenger side wheels resting on the edge of a storm ditch. I knew this ditch was about eight feet deep and full of rainwater, making it virtually a creek. My cruiser leaned so far over that the driver's side wheels were off the ground, and each time I tried to move, I felt the cruiser rocking toward the ditch.

I sat still for a moment then reached over and placed the radio microphone over the driver's side opened door window. Then I slid out of the seatbelt and very carefully and slowly, propped myself up over and out the driver's door window so I'd be hanging out far enough to keep the cruiser from rolling upside down in the water-filled ditch. I didn't want to chance climbing out the car window and have the gear on my gun belt get hung up, trapping me inside. At this point, I was able to grab the radio and request assistance.

In a moment my portly (I'm being kind) sergeant drove up, looked over at me hanging halfway out the car window, and said, "Joe, that's not a very good place to park your cruiser."

I just rolled my eyes and said, "Shut up, fat ass, and get me out of here."

9

Rescue at Your Own Risk

Heroism is opportunity.
It is a moment of exhilarating human experience that all men
dream about, but relatively few are ever fortunate enough to be
in the right place at the right time to experience and demonstrate
their loyalty to a magnificent phenomenon—human life.

I was sixteen years old when I experienced my first opportunity to save a life. My buddy, Enrique (Hank) Hernandez, and I were stopped at a stop sign preparing to turn left onto Hempstead Turnpike in our hometown of Elmont, Long Island. At that particular intersection, Hempstead Turnpike was at the top of a hill. Just to our right, a parked car on Hempstead Turnpike began rolling backwards. As it passed in front of us, I jumped out of the driver's seat and began chasing the runaway car. I spotted a woman in the car's path, pushing a baby carriage.

She was on the street, standing just off the curb in front of a parked car. Her head was turned in the opposite direction watching for oncoming traffic. No matter how loudly I yelled, she couldn't hear me over the roar of traffic on the turnpike.

Catching up with the car, I managed to get the driver's side door open, dove in headfirst, grabbed the steering wheel with my right hand and slammed on the brakes with my left hand, then set the emergency brake. Hearing a woman's scream, I looked up to see the mother grasping her baby carriage. She was stunned but very grateful.

I started the car and drove it back up to its original parking space. Just as I pulled up, the car's owner appeared. Spotting me alongside his car, he grabbed me, thinking I was stealing it. Fortunately, there were several witnesses who stepped forward to inform the owner what we did and chastised him for not securing the emergency brake. He apologized, somewhat embarrassed.

Several days later, Hank and I were leaving a movie theater in Freeport. It was late night and walking past a parked car, we noticed the headlights on. Without saying anything, our first thought was to open the car door and turn off the headlights. Our second reaction prevailed. We turned and looked at each other simultaneously, shaking our heads no and continued on home.

*

Of the three shifts-days, evenings, and midnights—the least contact the patrol shift commander will have with the outside world is between midnight and 8:00 AM. The only other person on duty in the patrol office is the administrative officer, who screens all incoming phone calls and assists walk-in citizens with complaints or problems. One benefit for the captain working the midnight shift was the opportunity to catch up on paperwork and stay up to date reading the latest law enforcement periodicals. But from time to time, things did happen in the office even at that hour.

One night, the administrative office man, Corporal John Oliva, was leaning against my doorway; and we were chatting about current police happenings. The phone rang; and John, instead of walking back to his desk, walked a few feet to the doorway access between the captain's and lieutenant's offices and answered that phone. In less than a minute and with a concerned and puzzled look on his face, John motioned to me to pick up the phone.

The voice on the other end was weak and unintelligible. Not too infrequently, drunks and other irate individuals would call to complain or cuss at the police and we would hang up. In this case, we felt we needed to listen because the caller might have been in trouble; and in a moment, we concluded the caller was an elderly female.

We maintained phone contact, trying to learn her location. If she hung up or we otherwise lost contact, it would take hours, if not days, for the phone company to run down the location of that phone. We continued asking, "Where are you? What is your address?"

Finally, we received enough information to determine that she was in a housing project. But she gave us a street address that didn't exist in any Tampa housing development. Without giving up and after repeated questioning, we realized that she wasn't in Tampa. Why then was she calling the Tampa Police Department?

I detected the lady was tiring and her voice, already very weak, was getting weaker; and I was afraid we were going to lose her. Suddenly, she told us she was in Miami! Without disconnecting, we got Miami PD on another line and relayed the information. In less than a minute, a Miami police officer was on the phone talking to me. When he got the call from his dispatcher, he was just leaving an apartment near the lady in need.

What were the odds? According to the Miami officer, this was a lady in her nineties, living alone. She had fallen several days earlier and could not get up but finally managed to crawl to the phone. The puzzling thing was why did she call the Tampa Police? Why didn't she call the Miami Police?

I learned via the Miami officer that she was trying to call her sister in Georgia when she hooked up with us. We learned that her sister's phone number was one digit off on the area code and one digit off our office phone number. Now what were the odds of that happening?

Every time I think about that phone call, I think of how quickly we could have just hung up the phone on what we believed was just another drunk. So many times, just taking that extra step pays off. In this case, Corporal John Oliva took that extra step.

*

As a patrol sergeant one busy Friday night, I was running from one call to the next, either backing up one of my officers, or on serious business showing up to evaluate and determine if my officer(s) needed anything to complete their investigation.

While at an officer's call, I would pick up any reports he had completed. I heard my downtown unit call for a wrecker and the paddy wagon—a DUI arrest. The arresting officer and his backup were on Ashley Street in front of the Convention Center. Taking the Ashley Street I-4 exit and approaching the scene, I noticed that both officers, engaged in conversation, were leaning against a cruiser right behind the drunk driver's car. The paddy wagon had not yet arrived at that location, so I was expecting to see the driver in the rear seat of the arresting officer's cruiser. I pulled up behind the backup officer's cruiser and approached the two officers.

Curious about who is being arrested, I peered into the cruiser but there was no prisoner. I looked up and spotted the driver, still seated in the driver's seat of his car. Surprised, I looked over at the officer; and before I could ask, he said, "It's okay, Sarge, I have his keys—he's not going anywhere except jail."

I said, "Well, that makes no difference. The prisoner should be handcuffed and in the backseat of your cruiser."

I walked over to the driver. He was rocking slightly and his hands were shaking, even though he was gripping the steering wheel. I leaned in close to the driver's window and picked up a strange odor.

"Oh, shit!" I yelled.

Both officers jumped and ran over. I said, "I think this man is a diabetic! Get the medics out here! Call an ambulance! Quick!"

Fortunately, Tampa General Hospital was just a few blocks away. Our subject was in diabetic shock but survived.

I remember a young officer on his first night assigned to the paddy wagon. When he arrived at the booking desk and opened the back door to the wagon, he found a dead prisoner. He felt very badly. I consoled him, saying it wasn't his fault. There wasn't any reason to believe the prisoner was near death or even sick when he was picked up.

I added, "Don't worry, the odds of you having that happen again to you is almost nil."

Well, that was the wrong thing to say. In less than a month, it happened to him again.

*

One night, when I was a patrol sergeant, I responded to the downtown Greyhound bus depot on a suspicious package, possibly a bomb. The officer on the scene was attempting to gain more information from the ticket clerk who overheard a white male talking about a bomb in one of the public storage lockers. There were only a few people in the waiting room. I directed all patrons to leave the bus depot as we suspected a bomb might be somewhere on the premises.

An elderly lady who looked a lot like Ma Kettle was grinning from ear to ear, carrying a cloth bag full of clothes and was all excited about what was happening. Apparently, something like this back in her hometown would have been considered a spectacular, once-in-a-lifetime event.

She wore a straw hat with a small artificial flower looped up over the top, a long cotton dress, and stockings rolled down to her ankles. If she ever had any teeth, she either swallowed them or they all just fell out over the years. She at first pretended to leave, but soon she had inched her way back inside. In the meantime, we were all too preoccupied to pay any more attention to her.

At this point, we didn't really believe there was a bomb anywhere. Bomb calls were a common happening, with few, if any, true bombs ever located. After checking about six or seven lockers, we opened one containing a large brown paper bag. One of the officers just reached in and began to lift an article out, and we got quite a surprise. We stood for a moment gaping at a cigar box with wires protruding out and attached to several flashlight batteries taped to the exterior of the box.

Someone blurted out, "Oh, shit, bomb!" When the old lady heard the word "bomb," she jumped out of her shoes, her hat flying off as she leapt over furniture. Out the door she went, gone and never to be seen again. Not by us, anyway.

Once the building was cleared, I suggested raising the box lid to peek inside; passing that test, we could then cut the wires. However, after a brief discussion, we decided we needed the department's bomb expert, a detective.

We learned he would not respond unless authorized by a commander. This night a senior sergeant was the acting shift commander. He notified the on-call division commander, who responded to the scene and said, "Yeah, that looks like a bomb. Have that expert detective respond."

Gee, I was so glad that brilliant division commander came out to confirm we had a suspected bomb on our hands. I would have never been able to determine that all by myself!

By now, it was about midnight and the expert detective arrived, looked over the cigar box, raised the lid, and peeked inside. After cutting the wires, he said goodbye. "I'll make my report tomorrow."

Boy! A double whammy! A brilliant commander and a superior bomb expert!

Speaking of bombs, when I was patrol sergeant arriving for duty one afternoon at approximately 2:15 PM, Major Jim Diamond called me into his office. I couldn't determine if he was frustrated, angry, or both, but knowing Jim, it was probably both.

He related the following to me: police communications received a call at approximately 1:00 PM from a City Hall employee who stated they might have a bomb in or near the mayor's (Dick Greco's) office.

Major Diamond said, "Joe, get down to City Hall and find out what the hell is going on. I can't get any information from anybody, and it seems the supervisor and officers on the scene are just running around scratching their heads and not getting any answers."

To this day, I don't know why Big Jim decided to send me to City Hall when he had another supervisor on the scene. Anyway, I made it there in less than five minutes and headed straight for the mayor's office, walking right past the secretary who blurted out, "Hey, you can't just go in—"

When I opened the door to his office, my first words were "Afternoon, Mayor," and nodded to several men seated in front of his desk.

Mayor Greco smiled and said, "Come on in."

I said, "Mayor, this place is buzzing with news of a bomb in your office, and I want you out of here right now."

Dick laughed and placed his hand on my shoulder, trying to compose himself while his two visitors sat looking at us, perplexed.

I cut the mayor off with "Mayor, I have an irate division commander waiting for my findings, and I'm more afraid of him than I am of you."

Dick stopped laughing momentarily to enlighten me as to what had happened. It seems he had been standing in a hallway of City Hall, chatting with a member of his staff, explaining he had to fly out to New York later in the evening, and because he didn't like to fly, he'd probably be *bombed*. A young female worker was turning the corner of the hall when this was being said, and by the time she told several other employees and they told several other employees, the story turned into "The mayor is going to be bombed," and then to "There is a bomb in City Hall."

Major Diamond couldn't understand why I was laughing when I called to brief him on the issue. He was not one to laugh, chuckle, or even smile when serious issues were being discussed. Oh well. I still always liked Big Jim. You always knew where you stood with him, and he didn't respect anyone who was afraid to question him. But if you had the moxie to do so, you had better be right.

*

One night on the midnight shift, I was working patrol zone 7, which is about midway in the city from all directions. B. J. Anderson was in zone 8. Working my way east on Hillsborough Avenue, checking storefronts, I spotted B. J. stopped at Twenty-second Street for a red light. He was in direct line with my headlights. I flashed them on and off rapidly. He saw me, and we pulled up driver's side to driver's side under a canopy at a gas station. The radio was unusually quiet as we chatted.

Suddenly, Officer Rolla Standau was screaming over the police radio, "ZONE 10! ZONE 10! I'M IN PURSUIT OF TWO BLACK MALES SOUTH BOUND OF FLORIDA AVENUE."

Even though patrol zones 9 and 20 were competing for radio air space, yelling over the radio at the same time, we could still make out that they were responding to back up zone 10.

BJ said, "You can go, but I'm going to stick around here because if we both respond, the closest patrol unit to our adjoining areas is downtown, several miles away."

I quickly headed up toward Sulfur Springs. Officer Standau was very excited, and it was difficult to make out what he was yelling over the radio. We knew he was somewhere on Florida Avenue and Bird Street, just a block from the Hillsborough River. At about eighty to ninety miles per hour, I headed north on Florida Avenue. Approaching Bird Street, I saw Standau out on foot, chasing the suspect toward the river. I turned onto a dirt roadway, more like a beaten path, also toward the river.

I could hear patrol units buzzing all around on both sides of the river, and I spotted an officer's flashlight along the riverbank. Officer Ken Maskrey was using his flashlight and listening to the splashing water, trying to find Standau, who by now was in the middle of the river, yelling for help.

Standau's objective had changed from trying to catch a couple of thieves, (the car they were driving was stolen) to a rescue mission. He was trying desperately to rescue one of the suspects. We could hear Standau but could not see him. Officer D. J. Halligan reached the shoreline just before I did and was jumping in the water when I pulled up. All he shed was his gun belt, otherwise he was fully clothed.

I've been submerged in the water fully clothed—not a good situation to be in. I stripped down to the waist and headed out, following the sound of splashing water and voices. D. J. found Standau but now was so tired he couldn't pull him to shore. I followed D. J.'s voice and told him to keep talking so I could find him.

Finally, I made it to his location about midway in the river, which at this point is about thirty yards wide. D. J. was exhausted, but because he had hastily jumped in the river, he was successful in finding Standau before he drowned. However, Standau was now unconscious, and D.J. couldn't bring him to shore. There was no time to tread water and rest because Standau could have died.

I grabbed Standau and headed for the shoreline, telling D.J. to stay close behind me. I couldn't see him and continued yelling out, "D.J., are you there?"

Gasping, he responded, "Yeah, right behind you."

It was dark, and we couldn't see the shore. We heard officers on both sides of the riverbank, but I had trouble understanding why they couldn't find us with their flashlights. As their voices grew increasingly fainter, I realized the strong current was carrying all three of us downstream, so I yelled as loud as I could, "LIGHTS! WE NEED SOME LIGHTS OUT HERE!"

Finally, I could see the shoreline; but by this time, we were exhausted, and it seemed like forever before we made it to shore. D. J. was flat out on the ground, exhausted. I immediately placed myself back against a tree in a sitting position, and I pulled Standau's back up against my chest. I grabbed him around his waist, clasping my hands together, and began the Heimlich maneuver. Water spurted out of his mouth by the quart, and after about six pulls, he began to cough and breathe. Standau was alive.

I was later told that Standau's father lost his life while he was a Tampa police officer. And only one week after President Kennedy was assassinated, Officer Standau was killed when a drunk driver struck him head-on while he was on his police motorcycle. It was the first police funeral that I attended. Unfortunately, it was not the last.

*

Police response to or happening upon house fires while on night patrol is not uncommon. As an officer on the street, it just seemed that there was always a fire somewhere nearby.

Once, when working the day shift as the shift commander (acting captain), I asked my partner, Lieutenant Diecidue, to cover the office while I went to lunch. Once on the street, I received a message to return a phone call. While conversing in a phone booth on the corner of North Boulevard and Cypress Avenue, I looked west down Cypress and observed a large area of sky, dark with thick black smoke.

It was a house fire. This was a black neighborhood between downtown and west Tampa. Both sides of the street were lined with small wood-framed shotgun houses. They were so close together you could stand on the fence between them and almost touch the roof eaves of the houses on either side of you.

Approaching the fire, I could see the paint on a parked patrol car melting and peeling off—the fire was burning that intensely. But there was no time to concern myself about that. There is no good day for a fire; but this particular day the wind was blowing, and the fire was moving quickly down the row of houses. People were grabbing anything they could and running from their homes. The flames were spreading house to house so quickly it looked like someone was brushing the flames on with a huge paintbrush.

I heard a young male voice, yelling, "Grandpa, Grandpa!" I spotted the boy, who looked to be about sixteen years old, running down between two houses. I ran after him, and as he reached a doorway halfway toward the rear of the house, he was still yelling for his grandfather. He began to enter the house when I grabbed him by the belt, pulling him back, and I had to hold him to prevent him from going inside. The interior was filled with thick black smoke.

You couldn't see more than a few feet inside the house. The roof was ablaze, but for some reason, this kid knew his grandfather would try to reach a bedroom on the side of the house. I jumped up on the fence between the houses, leaned forward with both hands on the windowsill, which was about five feet off the ground, and began yelling for the old man. Finally, I spotted a gray head coming through the bedroom doorway. I yelled inside for the old man to come toward me. I reasoned that if he could hear me, he could follow my voice from the doorway. I decided to jump onto the window's exterior frame.

When I jumped, my ribs got there first, knocking the wind out of me; but I hung on. Looking up at the roof, I knew I hadn't much time. The heat was very intense, and I was breathing heavily after hurting my ribs. I continued to yell for the old man to come to me. He was crawling slowly along the floor, but finally, he made it to the window. I bent over into the window opening, reached down, and with both arms, I grabbed him around the waist.

By this time, he was either semiconscious or unconscious. In either case, I couldn't pull him up and out because he was, for all intent and purposes, deadweight; but the officers outside the window—Burgess, McAllister, and Hathon—all grabbed me and pulled both of us out. They then dragged us away from the house—which by this time was totally engulfed in flames.

We both ended up in the hospital emergency room. While I was lying there in the hallway, a black lady approached me and thanked me for saving her father. She was somewhat surprised to learn I was a police officer. Fire department commanders wore white shirts with dark blue uniform pants, which were actually identical to the police lieutenant uniform.

My ribs really hurt badly, but I never revealed this to the doctors. After talking to me, satisfied I was okay, they released me. I maintained my silence about my ribs because I was flying to New York the next night for my kid sister Susan's wedding. I had made her a promise to be there; of course, she threatened to kill me if I didn't show up.

When I flew back to Tampa several days later, I caught up on some sleep and then reported for duty to work the midnight shift. Entering my office, I noticed a polished brass police hat badge in my in-basket. Apparently, when I had jumped onto the windowsill at the fire, my hat had fallen inside.

The captain told me the old man had come by the day before with the hat badge. He had found it in the aftermath of the fire, polished it, and came by to return it to me. I sat in the office that night, visualizing the old gent rummaging through his burned-out home and finding the remains of a police hat with the word LIEUTENANT inscribed on the hat badge—a badge badly marred by the fire. He had taken the time to clean it up, polish it, and return it to me. It was his way of saying thank you for what I had done. Thank you for being there when I knew I was going to die.

Over the years, citizens had expressed their appreciation for assistance that officers rendered. I had received letters of commendation for a number of incidents, but this really touched me. I thought about it all night.

To this day, I remember what that man did to express his appreciation for saving his life. I'll always regret never seeing him again. But in the end, there is no level of recognition more rewarding than knowing you laid it on the line and saved a human life. It's a sense of worth and satisfaction that will stay with you for your entire life, and I know that officers Burgess, McCallister, and Hathon felt the same way.

*

About a year later, I arrived on the scene of another house fire, a two-story blaze and screams coming from within. The fire department had not yet arrived, and there wasn't much of a chance of making an entry to attempt rescue. Anyone within that house was not possibly going to survive.

However, on the north side of the house, a black male was hanging upside down from a second-story window—his leg pinned by the window, which had apparently dropped down as he made an attempt to jump or climb out of it. He was just hanging there, yelling for help. Smoke was bellowing out all the windows, but with no ladder, we couldn't reach him.

Corporal Jim Yates yelled, "Where the hell are the fire trucks? They've got ladders!"

We couldn't wait any longer. Corporal Yates was a good-sized man, quite broad in the shoulders. I climbed up on his shoulders, reached, and grabbed the man's hands and pulled. After several tugs, he broke loose from the window, came down on top of me, and then Yates went down. Striking my head on something, a leg or the ground, I was momentarily dazed.

Guiding me away from the house, Yates shook me, which sure didn't help with the pain, and asked, "Joe, are you okay?"

I said something like "Just give me a minute."

Within a moment I was able to approach the house and rejoin Yates and the other officers who arrived on the scene. We spotted an elderly black male who had made it to a second-floor porch. He seemed confused and either couldn't hear or ignored our yells for him to jump. The drop wasn't that high, and if he had jumped, he surely would have survived, especially if we had broken his fall. But he was surrounded by the intense heat of the fire and suddenly burst into flames. A fireman laddered up and brought him down.

I ended up in the emergency room again with a tremendous headache. The elderly man who was now across from me was moaning and in obviously great pain. When I looked over, all I saw was raw flesh from his neck around his shoulders and his ears. The doctor signaled that the man would not survive—and he didn't. Several other people died in that fire as well. The man hanging from the window survived, but I was told he lost his leg below the knee.

I've never seen a monster or horror movie that could compare with what I witnessed—human beings trapped in a fire screaming, burning to death, still alive but with their skin gone, flesh exposed, in great pain and dying. You never forget these experiences. I can only imagine what soldiers go through during times of war. I don't believe I've ever viewed World War II veterans who could describe their experiences without becoming visibly emotional. I understand why.

*

One night while my wife, Alice, and I were dining at a favorite steakhouse, Alice began choking, grasping her throat with both hands. She was on the verge of passing out, when I jumped up out of my chair and immediately applied the Heimlich maneuver. On the second or third pull, a hardened piece of steak landed on the table. Although somewhat embarrassed, she managed, with my encouragement, to maintain her dignity.

I never had the opportunity to be trained in or practice the Heimlich maneuver, but just reading about it and keeping the procedure in mind, I applied it successfully. Ironically, two ladies who were dining at the next table over introduced themselves as nurses, stating they were about to step up and apply the maneuver themselves until they saw me react to the emergency.

Though we continued dining, I realized I could have lost Alice. We had been married since 1978. She was almost my hometown girl. She grew up just blocks away from me in Bay Ridge, Brooklyn; but she attended Catholic school and I attended public school, so we never had the opportunity to meet.

Just after we were married, a friend asked, "Joe, knowing what you know now, if you could go back and start life all over, what would you do differently?"

I didn't hesitate in answering that question. I responded, "I'd go back and look for Alice."

Alice is the greatest love of my life. When we met and fell in love, the job took second place. Seeing Alice for the first time, I was mesmerized by her beautiful eyes. Her dark curly hair surrounded a perfectly toned face, and her smile was gentle and innocent. She dressed with class, and her clothes perfectly fit her slim body.

I remember dancing with her one night at a cop's traditional hangout, Carmine's on Buffalo Avenue. I told her then that we would be married someday. I always remind her of her response, "Ha! No way!"

Ha to you, sweetheart.

10

The Street Cop's Lifeline

It takes a special kind of individual to be a good police dispatcher because the job brings with it a level of stress and frustration second only to the cop on the street. There always seemed to be a special bond between the street cops and the dispatchers.

Police dispatchers and other communications personnel make up one of the most critical police teams in local law enforcement. The police dispatcher is the street cop's lifeline.

In the communications work area, the call-taking section was separated from the dispatching section by a glass panel. Both tasks were interchangeable assignments among communications personnel.

At that time, most information and transactions from phone callers to call takers to dispatchers all required handwritten notes. The only computers utilized were limited to researching vehicle tag numbers and wanted persons. The call takers, receiving requests for the police via the telephone, would document pertinent information, such as time, location, complainants' names (if given), and the nature of the call on a statistically designed card. The card is then placed on a conveyor belt, which transported it from the outer call-taking counter under the glass partition to the dispatcher, who then provided the information to the patrol unit being assigned to the call. Those cards were then routed to the police records section to collate the information for research purposes.

There were two primary dispatchers handling patrol calls and activities: patrol district 1, the west side of town, and the eastside, patrol district 2.

As Tampa patrol officers, we were very fortunate because, overall, the department maintained competent and dedicated police dispatchers.

In spite of the traditionally negative employee stereotypes in any workplace, poor attitudes rarely surfaced when it came to officer safety on the street. Regardless of personal conflicts, dislikes, and disagreements, when it came to the cops on the street it was all one family and don't mess with the "kids!" Many times, officers, after handling an emergency or otherwise dangerous incident, expressed their appreciation for the way dispatchers handled it.

*

Most patrol officers ride solo, so the police dispatcher must act quickly, keeping track of several dozen patrol units on the street handling a wide variety of situations. Patrol units dispatched to a potentially dangerous incident—such as domestic violence, robberies, or burglaries in progress—are often able to coordinate a simultaneous arrival at the scene for officer safety purposes. However, officers patrolling frequently happen upon suspicious or illegal activities and initiate police action based on their own on-scene observations. When this happens, the officer's safety net is the police dispatcher.

*

My wife, Alice, began her career with the Tampa Police Department in 1973 as a switchboard operator in the communications section, then advancing to a police dispatcher.

Alice's forte, without a doubt, was her job as a police dispatcher. Once she mastered the job, she had the ability to keep track of every officer's location, always making sure backup was dispatched in potentially dangerous situations. If a patrol unit was out of radio contact for too long, she would automatically dispatch a backup.

*

In one such incident, Alice was dispatching when Officer Pinta advised, via the police radio, he was stopping a suspicious vehicle. Alice acknowledged his stop and said she would dispatch a backup unit. Pinta stated he would advise her if he needed one. However, Alice immediately dispatched a backup. Fortunately for Pinta, that she did. After getting off duty, he thanked Alice. Pinta told Alice that when he approached the suspicious car, he stopped the driver and several other males got out of the car, and he immediately sensed he was about to be attacked. However, at that moment the backup unit arrived.

*

In the late 1960s and early 1970s, clashes in black neighborhoods between the police and rabble-rousers (not the hardworking black residents) was not uncommon. Information gathered nationwide revealed cases of officers being set up responding to phony calls and then being ambushed.

One night, Alice, assigned to the call-taking section, received a call about a tree down across the road on Twenty-sixth Avenue, which was in the heart of a black neighborhood. For whatever reason, Alice had a gut feeling it was a setup. To this day, she could not tell you why. She was so sure of it; however, she had the responding units warned that this might be a setup and additional backup patrol units were quickly dispatched to the scene.

The patrol units responded from all directions, and as it turned out, it was a setup. However, because additional patrol units were dispatched to the scene, it was also a failed setup.

Alice could sit at the dispatch position for most of an eight-hour shift without a break. She was so engrossed in her work that days later, without any notes to refer to, she remembered information that both she and police units had transmitted over the police radio.

For instance, a detective once requested through the dispatcher, Alice, to talk to a patrol unit. The detective needed information about a car they had stopped days earlier, such as names, tag numbers, vehicle descriptions, etc. The officer paused and indicated he would check his notebook for the information. Alice broke in on the conversation and said, "I remember that," and began transmitting names, car descriptions, and tag numbers without referring to notes. You can imagine the surprise of the detectives and officers. This is a good indicator of someone very much involved in her work.

While sitting in the call-taking section, Alice once overheard another employee on the phone with a citizen. The employee seemed agitated with the caller. She stated that she couldn't understand the person, indicating that he must be drunk. Alice picked up the phone and began conversing with the caller. By being more inquisitive, she learned that the subject on the other end was a young retarded boy who needed help.

In another case, Alice received information over the phone about an abandoned Corvette parked at Tampa International Airport. For whatever reason, the airport police couldn't handle it, and there was no record of it being stolen. Alice, based on a caller's information, made several phone calls and learned it was a stolen car and dispatched a patrol unit to handle it.

There are far too many other stories involving the outstanding work by police dispatchers to print in this book.

*

Many of my comrades and I at TPD will always remember what Alice would say to the patrol units when signing off after her shift had ended. She would always add, "And all units, have a good night."

When I retired, many officers stated the loss was doubled and voiced their affection and gratitude to Alice as their dispatcher. I bet if they all had a choice to determine which one of us would have stayed on the job, the units would still be hearing, "And all units have a good night."

City of Tampa Police Department
Signal 14 Newsletter

Volume 4 Number 6   City of Tampa Police Newsletter   July/August 1988

Pictures from the Past

As we prepare to go into the new "911 System", you can see we've come a long way in the area of communications. This picture was taken back in 1936. You might wonder where the dispatcher is - it's obvious if you look at the time on the clock; the dispatcher has gone to lunch!

11

The Police and the Segregated South

Centuries of oppression, discrimination, and other social injustices do not evaporate at the stroke of a constitutional pen. Even though this nation reversed the defects in state laws decades ago, setting the stage for eliminating the legal aspect of discrimination, social discrimination lives on, and cultural differences thwart society's efforts to totally eliminate bigotry.

The segregated South was an eye-opener for me. The most striking phenomenon I experienced as a military man, then as a young police officer, was the issue of race. Black people were neither respected nor treated as equals to white citizens.

I found it very difficult to accept both legal and illegal mistreatment of black citizens. Even black Tampa police officers were not treated as equals to their white counterparts.

*

My first experience with the segregated South was in 1955 when I flew down from New York to MacDill Air Force Base. I could not believe the way black people were treated: segregated bus stations, sitting only in the back of the bus, no eating at restaurants with white folks, separate water fountains in public facilities, state law forbidding interracial marriages. There was even a separate hospital for black people: Tampa Negro Hospital.

One evening at about midnight, I was waiting for the last bus back to MacDill Air Base when a black airman I knew walked up. We didn't work together but were in the same squadron. We began talking and laughing.

When the bus arrived, I followed him to the rear and sat down with him. The bus driver turned and said to me, "Hey! You get up front with the white folks."

I replied, "No. I'm staying back here with my friend."

After a brief argument, my friend said, "Joe, get your ass up front before we both get in trouble."

Being angry, stubborn, and young, I refused. But when a police officer happened by and made it clear I would have to move or go to jail, I finally, and reluctantly, moved.

Try to visualize a black Tampa police officer, in uniform on his way to work, using a public bus line, forced to get on the bus and walk past vacant seats in the white section because he is compelled by law to sit in the back. He'd have to pass white passengers he was expected to place himself in harm's way to protect, people who wouldn't give him the right time of day. How degrading and demoralizing that must have been!

The City of Tampa offered a Firemen & Police (F&P) Pension Plan. By the standards of the day, it was a very good pension plan. However, I learned early on in my career that black Tampa police officers were not allowed in the F&P Plan—the ultimate slap in the face. They could only apply for the general city pension plan, which offered significantly less in benefits. I found it difficult to comprehend this gross unfairness.

There were six or seven black officers on the department who were only assigned to black neighborhoods. As a rule, they did not ride with white officers, and there were no black police supervisors. Their bitterness at times was evident.

*

How the hell do you address a full-grown man as boy? During my first year as a rookie cop, some veteran officers voiced their strong objections to the way I approached black people. I treated them with the same respect as I did white people.

I'll never forget Mom saying to me, "Joe, you treat everybody with respect, black or white, no matter their religion and nationality. Don't judge people."

So I addressed black individuals with respect. *Yes, sir. No, ma'am. Mr. or Mrs. So-and-so.* Did I ever get angry and blurt out something derogatory? Hell, yes. Bad things are blurted out in the heat of the moment when you're getting your ass beaten. But I always felt sorry about it afterward.

The older cops would say, "If you treat blacks with respect, they will think they have the *upper hand.*" I never bought that bullshit.

*

In the late 1960s, black officers were integrated with their white comrades in the patrol division. Prior to this change, I can only recall one black detective—Sam Jones, Sr. I met Sam one night while working downtown in patrol zone 1.

It was 1961, I was still on probation, and my senior partner was one of the most indecisive people I have ever met. This particular night we were investigating an aggravated assault. We arrived at the scene, which was an apartment house in a black neighborhood. The victim, an elderly black male amputee, was being loaded into the ambulance. According to witnesses, the suspect, the victim's roommate—a much younger black male—stabbed the old man because he refused to hand over his Social Security check. While interviewing witnesses, we were advised via the police radio that the victim had expired at Tampa General Hospital. My partner, while very dependable and brave in physical confrontations, could not deal with any stressful or complicated situations.

I called for the sergeant, who never seemed to be available unless you could catch him traveling to or from the local coffee shop. The police dispatcher must have realized my dilemma and suggested I request a detective.

"Yes, that's it. Send me a detective," I said, gratefully.

Detective Sam Jones Sr. was a man you immediately liked when you first met him, and that feeling stayed with you. Sam walked me through the investigative process. He was ultimately one of the first black sergeants on the department.

We moved into the new police building, just north of the downtown area, at 1710 Tampa Street in July of 1961. What smacked you right in the face when you walked into the main public lobby area were the separate water fountains, one marked White and the other Colored. I used to razz some of the older southern officers by walking over and drinking from the black water fountain. As they passed I would say, "No"—and pause as if I was thinking, then shake my head—"tastes just as good as the white water fountain." Most guys laughed and shook their heads, though some were obviously agitated by my antics.

In the eyes of most blacks, the police were the enemy. You had to appreciate a black police officer. Not only was he discriminated against by his employer, but he was also shunned by many in the black community.

*

In 1978, as a captain, I was transferred from the Tactical Division back to my previous assignment: patrol district 2.

On my first day back, I set up my office items in the district 2 shift commander's desk. This office and the one desk in it were shared by all three captains: day, evening, and midnight shifts. I was welcomed back by several sergeants, officers, and one of my lieutenants. While seated behind the desk, conversing with others, I noticed a grid map of the east side of town (district 2) on a letter-sized sheet of paper pinned to the bulletin board adjacent to the desk. It had been colored with crayons.

I was taken aback when I noticed the title of the map at the top of the page in large black capital letters: DISTRICT TWO—"LITTLE AFRICA." Several officers, including a lieutenant, chuckled, but the room fell silent when I tore it off the bulletin board and pitched it in the wastebasket.

Someone remarked, "Oh boy, I know a lieutenant who's going to be mighty mad about this."

I responded, "We have a number of black police officers assigned to this district. I wonder how they feel about this map. I'll go toe-to-toe with anyone who has a problem with my discarding the map."

The next day, it was close to 2:00 PM and a Wednesday, the designated day for the district staff meeting with the division commander: the major.

All district captains and lieutenants were required to attend these weekly meetings. In the hallway approaching the captain's office, I could hear chatter, recognizing a number of voices. Then one obviously angry voice boomed out about the missing "Little Africa" grid map.

I turned the corner into the office and stated, "I took down the map. It was degrading to the black members of our department and sends the wrong message to the black community."

At about that time, the major walked in and asked what the argument was about.

Lieutenant Map-happy said, "Err, nothing boss, just shoptalk."

The meeting began, and there was no more conversation about inappropriate grid maps.

*

As colonel of operations (deputy chief), recognizing the black recruitment dilemma, I recall trying to generate a plan to recruit black citizens as police officers. I thought that by requesting help from the black clergy I would be successful. One black officer smiled at me and said only, "Good luck." So I made arrangements to speak at a gathering of black ministers to enlist their assistance.

I believed if they could encourage young men and women to join, blacks would be better represented in the police department. They could truly say it was *their* police department too.

I certainly became educated during this endeavor. The black ministers, as I spoke, were obviously uncomfortable, nervous, and tried not to acknowledge my presentation. I learned they had no intention of going to *their* people and promoting the department by asking black men and women to join. In fact, as I began my presentation, they gave me a time limit of five minutes to speak; and they cut me off when my time ran out.

Frankly, they visualized losing their position in the black community by supporting the enemy: the police. That was one reason it was difficult to recruit a sufficient number of black officers in the 1960s and 1970s. Today, the private sector has much to offer, and police agencies are still competing with them for black recruits.

By sheer numbers alone, it's a frustrating endeavor. Think about this: the average community has about a 12 to 14 percent black population. Only about 10 percent of all applicants, regardless of race, will meet the basic requirements simply to be selected for the job. Then they must successfully pass the academy curriculum. You'll probably lose 10 to 20 percent in the academy. Then they must survive field training, which is twelve to sixteen weeks on patrol, being trained by a certified field (police officer) instructor. At this point in the process, you could lose another 10 or 15 percent.

The last hurdle is completing the yearlong probationary period before being accepted as a permanent member. With approximately eighteen thousand police agencies in the nation competing for high-quality candidates, these figures should illustrate why we never stopped looking for recruits. It was difficult enough just to maintain the department's authorized strength of police officers.

It's rare indeed for many agencies to maintain full strength for longer than a few months. Many police agencies throughout the country are in a perpetual state of recruitment. This includes recruits of any race, nationality, and gender. When you consider the minority population ratio to the overall low percentage of acceptable police candidates and the competitiveness among police agencies to recruit minorities, does it not illustrate the difficulty to succeed in such a selective recruitment effort?

It is a flawed perception that police agencies are not actively recruiting minorities to be police officers. Keep in mind, the requirements and standards mandated for police candidates in most, if not all states, cannot be met by the majority of those who apply for a position in this profession. For obvious reasons, honesty and other personal traits, ethics, background, and psychological and physical fitness of all police candidates, regardless of race, are essential characteristics to be accepted as a police officer.

The men and women selected for police work are empowered to take away citizens' individual freedoms and, at times, unfortunately, their very lives.

*

Looking back at police attitudes, I believe most of us were not bigoted, but I do think there was a degree of insensitivity and ignorance on our part.

We were always dealing with the lowest elements of the human race, both white and black. The black culture was foreign to most of us. I believe these conditions aggravated and influenced our perceptions of black people. Their culture was different; and human nature, being what it is, our immature thinking was prejudicial. They ate different food, enjoyed different music, dressed differently, and spoke differently.

Frequently, police encounters with black people were met with resentment, anger, indifference, and suspicion. The prevailing attitude was that the police weren't your friends. Why should they have thought any differently?

I rolled up on a traffic accident late one night being investigated by a traffic officer. There were two motorists involved, one black and the other white.

The investigating officer could not determine who was at fault, so he stated, "Oh well, I'll cite so-and-so. He's just a nigger, anyway."

And we wondered why so many blacks perceived us as the enemy?

*

Another incident involved a black citrus farmer who was experiencing the theft of his crop. His farm bordered the eastern end of the city limits with Hillsborough County. When the farmer noticed tire tracks in one corner of his farm, he realized someone was driving into his groves late at night and stealing truckloads of oranges and grapefruit. It was obvious this had been going on for several weeks. He called the police, who advised him to stake out the grove and call back when he caught the thieves.

Well, he did just that. He hid out in the grove, accompanied by his young son. Sure enough, it wasn't long before a pickup truck with no headlights on slowly entered the grove one Saturday night. Two white men started loading the truck. The farmer confronted them at gunpoint and directed his son to run back to the house and have his mother call the police.

Later on that night, I entered the office and observed a handcuffed black male old enough to be my father sitting in a chair, quietly crying. The two officers who answered the theft call had just submitted their report to the sergeant.

After reading the report, the sergeant jumped up yelling, "What the hell did you two do?"

It seemed our two brilliant super sleuths responded to the grove and observed the black farmer holding two white men at gunpoint. They had received information from the police dispatcher that a black farmer was holding two white men for stealing fruit from his grove, which is a felony. They decided the black farmer was guilty of displaying a deadly weapon in a threatening manner so they arrested him. The sergeant almost came unglued. I can't recall everything he said to them, but I must admit, I didn't hang around to listen.

It was no wonder why blacks did not trust us, why they hated us, why we were considered the enemy, why black leaders in the community were reluctant to assist us in recruiting black officers, why little black kids looked frightened when a police cruiser rolled by. No matter that there were many of us who smiled, waved, and said hi, these kids had already been indoctrinated to mistrust the police.

*

You knew what had happened when a black man was brought to the booking section with the back of both hands lacerated and swollen. He had made the mistake of running from the police. Knowing he was about to be caught, a black man would drop to his knees and place both hands around the back of his head to protect it from what was coming. "The Man" (the cop) would bang the back of the black man's head with a blackjack, even though he didn't pose a threat to an officer. It was the punishment for running.

I saw that treatment once but couldn't stop it. Officer Ronz* chased a black man who ran when he spotted the police cruiser. The black man, who ultimately realized he was about to be struck by the officer, dropped to his knees and placed both hands against the back of his head. Ronz aimed for the back of the man's head but struck his hands instead. After securing the man, Ronz made a feeble attempt to justify his actions.

My response was "If I couldn't bring that old man down without a weapon, I would turn in my badge. I've grappled with you on the mat, and you had to hit him because you can't fight worth a shit."

*

My wife, Alice, had a black female coworker when she was a Tampa police dispatcher in the 1970s. They enjoyed each other's company, lunched together, and conversed on the job. The coworker had a great sense of humor, enjoyed people, was intelligent, and liked her job.

One day, the coworker announced that she was selling her house, which was located in an all-white neighborhood. Alice picked up the tone in her voice and asked why she was selling as the coworker had only recently moved into that neighborhood with her husband and children.

She described her experience as a nightmare. Not one person in the neighborhood would even say good morning. Their snubbing made it obvious blacks were not welcome. The coworker was devastated. She really liked her home and the neighborhood but eventually moved out because her husband and, especially, the children were not welcome, and she knew they would not be accepted by the whites. She was very bitter about that treatment and understandably so.

After this, she did not want to mix with whites and be the object of rejection because of her darker skin. She just couldn't bring herself to take that risk again. Alice said from that day forward the coworker seemed reluctant to have lunch with her, make conversation, or engage in any social activity again. It wasn't long after that she resigned her position with the department.

*

I was told that in one small primarily white and affluent community, the police routinely received calls from local merchants when black consumers entered their stores. That's it—just by entering the store, panic ensued.

Instinctively the owner or clerk would call the police. "There are black people in my store," the clerk would say.

"Okay," was the police communications officer's response, "What are they doing?"

"Just walking around the store," the clerk would answer.

The dispatcher would respond, "Well, what's wrong with that?"

"They look suspicious," the clerk would retort.

And so it would invariably go.

*

Once, my wife, Alice, and her friend Mary Dickman were in a (white) neighborhood liquor store waiting in line, just before Christmas, when a large black male entered the store. Alice stated that he immediately recognized the discomfort of several white shoppers waiting in line at the checkout counter just inside the front entrance.

The owner came from the rear of the store at a fast pace and relieved his wife, who had been behind the counter. Alice said it was obvious to all, including the black man, that the owner was nervous. As it turned out, the black man was a cabdriver picking up his fare, an elderly white lady, standing in the same checkout line. It was a recurring scene for black citizens in almost all cases.

*

There were many good officers, including supervisors, who felt the same way I did about the mistreatment of black citizens. I remember a white officer assigned to the downtown walking beat on the day shift saving the life of a small black girl by breathing life back into

135

her little body. He never reported it because he was afraid he would be ridiculed by his fellow officers. However, before he even got off duty, his deed had become known. A greater number of officers came forward to praise him than anyone would have predicted.

*

Working the day shift on the north end, I stopped a car for a red light violation. The driver was a black man about fifty-five years old. I explained how I had observed him drive through the intersection against a red light and was issuing him a traffic citation.

As he handed me his driver's license, he said, "You're giving me a ticket just because I'm black."

I leaned closer to the driver's window, paused, and looked at him. I said, "Black drivers and white drivers run red lights every day, and both black people and white people are killed. So how do I justify letting you violate the law just because you're black?"

He didn't respond. But when I returned to his car to have him sign the citation, he looked up, handed me the signed citation, and said, "You're right, Officer, I was wrong."

Smiling, I replied, "Thank you, and you drive carefully now."

I hoped that this man would remember how I handled the incident and have a better perception of the police. While discriminatory treatment still prevails in our society, the police have come a long way in race relations today.

*

One night, we were posted at an intersection just north of an ongoing civil disturbance. We had stopped several people to obtain identification at the request of patrol units, observing them leaving the area. Each time we stopped two or three together, they were confrontational. At one point, after dealing with several groups, we were not in a good frame of mind to hear via the police radio that an officer had been injured and several had been shot at.

A black male wearing a straw hat approached us, crossing over to the other side of the street. At first, he ignored my order to stop and identify himself. Finally, realizing we meant business, he turned and walked over to us standing by the squad car.

His facial expression gave away his obvious anger, but he never spoke. He handed us an ID card—he was a marine on leave from Vietnam. This probably hadn't been the first time he had been stopped by the police that night.

Now I felt pretty bad. It was quiet momentarily, but then as I handed him back his identification, I extended my hand and said, "We're all somewhat edgy tonight, but it can't compare to what you've probably experienced in the war. I want you to know that I appreciate your dedication to our country."

He looked up at me, my hand still extended; and for a minute, I thought he would never grab it. He looked surprised, relieved, and full of pride all at the same time. Eventually, he did shake my hand, said thank you, and walked away. I watched as he left. When he was about thirty or forty feet away, he turned, looked at us, waved, and we waved back. How could a nation of free people turn their backs on black Americans who had fought for this country?

*

One evening, officers brought in a husband and wife for shoplifting at Montgomery Ward, where a bottle of men's cologne was allegedly stolen. The husband was a black man and a Clearwater police officer, and his wife was a white woman and a schoolteacher. The standard procedure in shoplifting cases was that the department store security detained the suspect(s) and called the police, who transports the arrestees to jail, and completed the reports. The department store was the arresting party; the police merely assisted.

The transporting officer expressed concern about this case. He felt that the arrest by the department store security personnel was flawed. The officer said that while he was placing the husband and wife in the paddy wagon, he overheard one of the store detectives make a racially derogatory remark about the mixed marriage. Being the on-duty shift commander, I interviewed the husband and wife.

They related the following:

While visiting in Tampa, they decided to shop for a unique men's cologne they couldn't find in their local stores. Finding it in Montgomery Ward, the husband carried it in his hand. While they continued to shop throughout the department store, he would set the cologne down while trying on clothes, etc. Being engrossed in conversation and not buying any other merchandise, they ambled out of the store, with the husband still carrying the cologne in plain view. They explained they were just absentminded but were arrested anyway. Surprisingly, their version of the story was confirmed by the Montgomery Ward security personnel!

I made contact with the Hillsborough county state attorney's office and explained to them, based on the circumstances (particularly the racial comments made by the store personnel), that the charges should be dropped—and they were. Several weeks later, the husband and wife paid me a visit to thank me. They handed me a small wooden plaque that reads—"FOR WHAT A MAN THINKETH . . . HE IS." This incident was one of many isolated happenings that left a black person feeling better about the police.

*

City governments, particularly police departments, had to take the lead to develop programs to improve police service and race relations on a community-wide scale.

But no program can take the place of the daily interaction police officers have with every citizen with whom they come into contact. It's up to each officer to project a professional image by treating each person with as much dignity as the situation will allow. When the opportunity presents itself, officers must always do whatever they can to assist people in their individual dilemmas as crime victims.

*

Throughout our nation, for decades, poor people have been offered, via government support, a place to live—housing projects. In Tampa, they were located in various areas of the city and were primarily occupied by black residents.

Patrolling the housing projects was routine. Domestic violence, fights, drugs, assaults, theft, rape, and property damage were frequent happenings; and patrol cars were a familiar sight in the projects. But during the civil rights movement, police entering the housing projects were met with resentment and at times, with rocks and bottles.

This resulted in very little willingness to patrol in the projects. Why go in there? The residents certainly didn't want us there. So our attitude was, we'll go in when answering a call and then quickly leave. When we did answer calls, very few residents would assist us, talk to us or come forth as witnesses. So what was the point?

I believe I was a captain when I finally realized the common belief that black housing project residents didn't want the police in their neighborhoods was wrong. "Thugs" didn't want us in there and made it difficult for law-abiding residents to assist us by using threats of violence to keep them apart from the police.

Hardworking black people, many of them single mothers, were afraid to speak out and say, "Please come into our neighborhoods." Being a single parent living in the projects amongst the criminal element had to be the most heartbreaking existence for a black mother trying to raise her children to be law-abiding citizens. Others, after years of discrimination and mistreatment, simply did not trust the police although they needed us. It was up to us to take the initiative and do something about the criminal element living and committing crimes in the projects.

This extended mistrust of the police compounded the failed race relations effort along with the department's struggle to attract qualified black people as police officers. The only possible response to bring about confidence and trust of black citizens had to be stimulated by police leadership.

In April of 1979, I was promoted to major (division commander) of one of the department's two patrol divisions. With a staff of dedicated commanders, sergeants, corporals, and police officers, we pioneered—I believe—the prototype of neighborhood policing, which I guess you could say was the grandfather of community policing.

Neighborhood policing wasn't Tampa's brainchild. It had been around for a few years in different versions, experimented with by police departments throughout many parts of the country.

A black man by the name of Askia Muhammad Aquil was very active in the Tampa black community. He was dedicated to improving the relationship between whites and blacks. When I met him, I liked him immediately. Considering the vast differences in our lives and backgrounds, we thought alike most of the time. He worked with me to develop the neighborhood-policing project. He never asked much for his dedication. I believe he loved his people very much, and just knowing somehow that he'd helped them was a great reward to him. He seemed to experience great personal satisfaction and a sense of achievement for his efforts in assisting us in fighting the illegal drug problem, primarily in the housing projects. He was never content with the status quo, and no matter how hard he worked, he felt he had never done enough.

Our plan specifically targeted housing projects. I had Captain Burt Hatcher coordinate the project. I directed him to research and submit the following information to my office:

1. Population of Tampa
2. Total population of all housing projects
3. Citywide (annual) crime rate
4. Annual crime rate in the identified housing projects

I learned the black housing projects consisted of approximately 7 percent of Tampa's population and experienced approximately 38 percent of the total crime in Tampa.

Armed with this information, we then discussed which housing project we would select for our experiment. We ultimately selected Riverview Terrace because its location was conducive to patrol assignments and geographically would augment our efforts to maintain constant patrol in the project area; thereby reducing the frequency of situations in the surrounding area requiring drawing patrol officers out of the project to handle calls. We chose to ask for volunteers rather than make it a mandatory assignment.

I was very pleased with the number of officers who volunteered to do this work. I made it clear this experiment was not without problems. There was concern about the reaction of residents in the project. But we did not dwell on that. We had enough experience to know people needed us and that we had an obligation to respond. Patrol officers would work in pairs and would only leave the housing project to respond to nearby emergency situations. Fortunately, there were very few instances requiring the patrol teams to leave their assigned areas.

Officers were oriented to

1. be good listeners;
2. knock on doors, telling people you were there to protect and help them; and
3. get out of the patrol car and stay on foot for the majority of the shift if possible.

They did all that and the response from the project residents was overwhelmingly favorable. People were inviting the officers into their homes for dinner. Within a matter of weeks, weekend calls and incidents dropped from approximately thirty-five to less than ten.

Several years later, the department had set up (police) substations in a number of housing projects. We were welcomed with open arms. Residents would help out at the substation and share their food with the police. In one case, officers were cheered by the residents when they escorted a rape suspect off to jail.

All this sent an important message to the criminal element. Unfortunately, in a few years, the substations were shut down because of the lack of funds. That sent a message to the criminal element too.

From left: (seated) Victor Buchanan, Willie Massey,
(standing) Romeo Cole Sr., Sam Brazelton,
James Roy Adams, Oscar Alcala, John Pounce,
Circa 1950's

12

The Spark and Energy of Riots

The civil rights movement in our nation brought into focus the image of many medium to large police agencies across the country. Trying to deal with the racial strife shed light on police deficiencies in both the upper command and individual officer levels of policing.

In almost all cases, the police were not prepared for such a movement. Just the small percentage of violent encounters demonstrated law enforcement's inability to cope with keeping the peace and enforcing the law. The use of force often catapulted the police into daily headlines in a negative way.

Faced with civil disobedience, our only choice was often the use of force. Formal crowd control, strategies, for the most part, simply did not exist.

Historically, it is thought there were two significant incidents, which were turning points in generating nationwide support for eradicating racial discrimination in our society. One occurred in Birmingham, Alabama, in 1963. What was described as a peaceful march led by Dr. Martin Luther King, Jr., was a revelation for many white Americans. The national news offered film of black demonstrators being attacked by police dogs. The police took this action under orders, according to some reports, by Police Commissioner Bull Conner, to turn the dogs loose on what was considered a peaceful crowd of black marchers.

The second incident was the 1964 murder of three civil rights workers in Mississippi. Even some of the officers who were staunch segregationists were in disbelief and voiced their disgust at the murders.

*

During the era of the civil rights movement, it didn't take much of an incident to ignite a riot. I had a difficult time accepting the wording that federal entities used to describe the rioting: "unusual occurrence." In one case, officers were impounding an abandoned disabled car. Why it was being impounded is not known. The point is, in calmer days, neither the police nor the residents of the housing project could have cared less whether a disabled car was parked on the street or being impounded. That was not an unusual occurrence.

However, anger was hanging over this community like a dark cloud ready to burst. Black citizens in Tampa became upset when arrests took place in their neighborhoods. Crowds would gather, shouting obscenities and threats. When a patrol car turned into the black neighborhood, particularly the housing projects, you could see the anger on people's faces. Their eyes followed you down the street. Crowds lingered not far from whatever the police were doing. All that was needed to ignite the fire was an instigator, a black activist bent on violence for the sake of violence. There were a sufficient number of agitators in every neighborhood.

When a wrecker arrived to pick up and tow a car or officers made an arrest, rocks, bottles, and obscenities flew through the air. Patrol cars would pour into the housing projects from every direction, and crowds of black citizens would shift from one street to the next, taunting police from alleys and throwing firebombs into buildings. Gunshots rang out everywhere.

The police believed the best thing to do was leave the area and not return until all was quiet. That worked for a while; but when the civil rights movement gathered more steam throughout the nation, in many cases, crowds turned into mobs that began burning and looting. When the police failed to react and take enforcement action against this riotous criminal conduct, it encouraged more mob violence and looting and burning. We realized we were not prepared to quell disturbances of such a magnitude. We lacked training, leadership, and plans for mob control.

*

During several days of civil disturbances, after a white officer shot a black man, I was working the evening shift training a new officer. At roll call, we were told there were disturbances in black housing projects on the east side of town. Most officers armed themselves with their own shotguns because the department didn't have enough of them. I borrowed a twelve-gauge double-barrel shotgun from another officer.

En route to our east side patrol zone, the police dispatcher dumped three or four calls on us. The calls pertained to broken car windows, with some involving injuries to drivers. White men and women employed at cigar factories in the Ybor City area were on their way home traveling northbound on Twenty-second Street, a local but main street running through black neighborhoods, including housing projects.

When they drove between Twenty-sixth Avenue and Lake Avenue on Twenty-second Street, bricks and bottles were being thrown by a mob of blacks at any car with white people in it. Police communications directed us to Fifteenth Street and Buffalo Avenue. When we arrived, we could see several cars and a taxicab parked with white people milling about, all with head injuries. We summoned paramedics for the victims. We could hear the police radio broadcasting information that motorists were still being attacked with bricks and bottles on Twenty-second Street.

I drove east on Buffalo Avenue, then turned south on Twenty-second Street, stopping and observing the street several blocks south of us littered with bricks, bottles, and beer cans. I eased into the area slowly, observing a large crowd of black people on the east side of the street in front of several storefronts, including a bar. As we passed, and I kept my eyes on the crowd, we bounced lightly over the littered street. I stopped directly in front of the crowd. There was loud laughter and catcalls.

When I stepped out of the cruiser, I walked slowly toward the crowd but no closer than about twenty feet. Not being the most graceful person in the world, I moved gingerly over the debris on the pavement, keeping alert. For a brief moment, there was dead silence. Someone in the crowd was saying something and moving toward the front. I unsnapped my holster and told my partner to call for some backup units. Then I realized my rookie partner was not behind me but still sitting in the passenger seat of the cruiser. I looked over at him, and it was obvious he had no intention of prying two yards of the leather car seat out of his ass to get out.

Walking toward the cruiser, I didn't take my eyes off the crowd nor did they take theirs off me. I eased behind the wheel, placed the cruiser in gear, and watched them until I was reasonably sure it was safe. I pulled across Twenty-second Street at Twenty-sixth Avenue, blocking northbound traffic.

Soon after, I was ordered to leave the area. I informed the police dispatcher of the danger to white motorists passing through the area and then moved further south and blocked northbound traffic at Columbus Drive on Twenty-second Street. Only black motorists, unless otherwise suspicious, were allowed to proceed north beyond Columbus Drive. After all, most of the black citizens were law abiding and most likely on their way home from work. It seemed like a long time had passed before the department mustered a sufficient number of officers to handle the disturbance north of us. Once in place, no traffic was allowed to proceed north.

Tampa had been inundated with news media people from all over the country, but most were from the Tampa Bay area. Learning the location of this particular disturbance, the media folks headed north on Twenty-second Street with their cameras and notebooks. I denied them access. Several came back a second and then a third time, and again they were denied access. Each time they failed to get by me, the angrier and more frustrated they became. By this time, the entire area had been sealed off.

My partner and I watched them leave. They parked and regrouped about a block south of our location. They were up to something. Sure enough, about twenty of them again approached us on foot, and again, we denied them access to the disturbance area.

One, acting as their spokesman, said, "You can't stop all of us."

Pointing my finger at the loudmouthed spokesman, I responded, "You're right. But you'd better believe you and the others close to you will be in two positions: First, facedown and handcuffed, then sitting in our patrol cars for the duration of this operation if you try to break this police line. And if you don't get off the street now, your ass will be locked up for violating the state's Media Civil Obstruction Statute."

They looked a little dumbfounded but turned, walked back to their cars, gathered, talked, looked back at us, then drove off.

My partner asked, "What's the state's Media Civil Obstruction Statute?"

I said, "I made it up, but it worked."

However, about ten minutes later, the shift commander via the police radio said, "Per the chief's orders, let the media people pass."

So much for keeping them off the street.

A rumor circulated the next day that reporters were paying black youths five bucks to throw rocks through car and business windows so they could get photos of it.

*

In May 1980, the McDuffie trial involved the death of a black man at the hands of police officers in the Miami area. After a high-speed motorcycle chase, McDuffie ended up dead. The allegations were that he was beaten to death by police officers when he was caught. It was also alleged that the officers involved falsified their reports to cover up the incident.

These officers were ultimately charged with his death. The news coverage in the Miami area enraged the black community, resulting in a change of venue for the trial, which was held in Tampa.

At that time, I was a division commander of Patrol district 2. The greatest number of black citizens lived in this patrol district on the east side of Tampa. The trial was brief, and so was the jury deliberation.

Verdict: not guilty. Results: a riot.

We mobilized and set up a command post on the fringe of those neighborhoods that would have the greatest need to control rioters. That meant deploying patrol units on the east side of Tampa between Nebraska Avenue east to Twenty-second Street and north from Broadway to Buffalo Avenue, a very densely populated area that included several housing projects with a large concentration of blacks. Though there would be civil disturbances in other areas, the east side would prove to be the biggest problem for the police.

A command post was set up on north Twenty-second Street, close to the housing projects. We anticipated a long weekend of disturbances, mostly by young black males. When calls came in of rioting or a gathering of people becoming unruly—throwing rocks at cars, setting dumpsters on fire, smashing storefront windows, and looting—patrol units would rendezvous and proceed into the area in force. We had undercover vice teams act as intelligence units. Driving civilian cars, wearing shabby clothes, and sporting beards, they could get closer and see more than marked patrols could.

This also gave us additional backup officers at the scene. At times police communications received bogus information about problem areas, a tactic used by troublemakers to divert police attention elsewhere. With vice units responding first and feeding information back to the command post, tactical decisions could be made more effectively by determining whether or not police units should be deployed and if so, how many, when, and what their tactical approach should be. We learned from experience not to deploy the fire department to dumpster fires because many times these were a ruse so rioters could pummel fire trucks and firemen when they arrived to extinguish the blaze.

We worked twelve-hour shifts. I would start at 6:00 PM, head straight to the command post, then head for the office, and change into my uniform.

At the command post, several blocks north of a housing project, calls started coming in from the police dispatcher about young black males gathering and becoming noisy and setting dumpster fires. The officers were geared up and ready to go. But I insisted on a report from undercover police units first. I refused to send in police units without first knowing that we were really needed. There was no point in deploying twenty or thirty officers to a gathering of noisy people or a dumpster fire that was not out of control or near a building.

Some officers, including sergeants and field commanders, were anxious to respond and subtly showed their disappointment in my decision not to *rush* in. I personally jumped in an undercover vice unit and directed them to take me into the so-called trouble area so I could see for myself. I ducked down because I was in uniform.

Going in to see for myself had several advantages. First, I could personally give the chief an accurate picture of what was happening. Second, it gave me a better picture and would influence my decisions for deployment of officers.

As I suspected, there was a large group of black males standing around, and one dumpster at a ball field was on fire but was not a threat to anyone or any homes, so I let it burn. There was no point in jeopardizing the firemen for that. Being selective in response to dumpster fires would discourage this tactic in the future. While there were a few skirmishes the first night, there were no reported serious injuries.

The next night—Wednesday, May 21, 1980—trouble broke out in the Robles Park housing project area. White motorists and police units traversing Lake Avenue were being pelted with rocks from blacks who would then duck back and conceal themselves in the projects. Patrol units were assigned to set up at Lake and Central avenues. This intersection was the southeast border of the Robles Park housing project. Northbound from the intersection on both sides of Central Avenue were housing projects and at least one bar on the east side of the street, which was always crowded with locals. The bar was a trouble spot for us. The areas south and west of this location were filled with single-family homes.

Once I was satisfied the operation was on track, I headed to the police station to change into my uniform. I always took pride in wearing it, no matter what my position or rank was.

Before changing into my uniform, I decided to stop by my office to make several phone calls. While on the phone, the police radio blared out—"OFFICER DOWN! OFFICER SHOT! CENTRAL AND LAKE!" I raced out to my staff car and headed back. I punched it up to over one hundred miles per hour on the interstate. When I arrived, paramedics were loading Officer Cooke into the ambulance. I walked up and looked down at Cooke. He was unconscious and had been shot in the face, just below eye level. I thought the worst—that he wouldn't make it.

I was looking around when somebody yelled, "Get down, there's a sniper!" I observed officers huddled behind police cars and storefronts. I crouched down and hustled over to a police car, knelt behind it, and recognized Special Agent Chambliss, a Florida Department of Law Enforcement agent, and a former Tampa police detective assigned to the tactical division at the same time I was. He was carrying a semiautomatic carbine.

I looked at him and said, "That may come in handy before this night is over." He acknowledged that.

Nobody was moving. We were situated on Central Avenue just a few feet south of Lake Avenue. Project apartments bordered the west side of the street and storefronts on the eastside. The main housing project area could be accessed through an alley (Nordica Street), located at the northwest corner of Central and Lake avenues. The Robles Park Lounge was on the east side of Central, north of Lake.

I got on the police radio and directed units to seal off the area around the housing project. All pedestrians and vehicles would be detained until we were reasonably satisfied they were not involved in the shooting of Officer Cooke.

I asked, "Where did the shot come from?"

Someone said, "I think it came from over there," pointing to the alleyway located just northwest of the intersection of Lake and Central avenues.

I decided to lead officers up the alleyway, which curved into Nordica Street, enter the housing project to begin searching the area and asking questions. I ordered the supervisor, who was responding with officers just north of us, to send several officers to cover the Robles Park Lounge and detain all patrons that were inside and in the parking lot.

As we entered the alleyway, a car occupied by several black people was leaving. Agent Chambliss thought he recognized the driver as one involved in the rock throwing just prior to the shooting of Officer Cooke.

Via the police radio, I ordered officers behind us to detain the driver and all passengers. Initially, the driver refused to stop and proceeded east on Lake Avenue. Again he was ordered to stop, which he did. Shortly after entering the housing project, I was told the driver of the car we ordered stopped was the shooting suspect.

Fortunately, Officer Cooke survived the gunshot wound.

The following day, one of my peers, another major, made the comment to our immediate superior, Colonel Bob Smith, that I had no business as a division commander getting involved in this incident. Bob voiced his disagreement, supporting my actions in this case.

I do know the officers involved in apprehending the suspect, as well as many others on the street that night, appreciated a top echelon commander responding and taking the initiative. It gave all of them a sense of pride in their police organization. I also felt a sense of pride because so many young officers stopped by my office and expressed their appreciation.

*

On October 24, 1996, TyRon Lewis—age eighteen years—was shot to death by St. Petersburg Police Officer James Knight. At the time I was police chief of Treasure Island, whose eastern boundary borders the city of St. Petersburg.

Officers James Knight and Sandra Minor stopped Lewis at Sixteenth Street and Eighteenth Avenue south, for reckless driving and speeding. The officers approached the driver's side. Lewis was driving, and another black male was in the front passenger seat. The car doors were locked, and the windows were heavily tinted, preventing the officers from any visual contact with the occupants.

THE SPARK AND ENERGY OF RIOTS

Lewis refused to roll down his window and refused to get out of the car, even after repeated orders to do so.

Officer Knight positioned himself in front of the suspect's car, drew his firearm and focused his attention on the driver, whom he could now see through the front windshield. Meanwhile, Officer Minor attempted to break a car window with no success. Lewis, the driver, drove forward, striking Knight several times and ultimately knocking him up onto the hood of the car. Knight, in self-defense, fired several rounds through the windshield, killing Lewis.

That night riots broke out in the predominantly black neighborhoods of South St. Petersburg, and the St. Petersburg police chief, via the countywide mutual aid agreement, requested police reinforcements from other municipal police agencies and the Pinellas County Sheriff's Office. I responded that night with five or six of my officers, teaming up with St. Petersburg patrol units, hitting trouble hot spots as needed.

At that point in time, very few of Treasure Island's finest had ever experienced an angry, riotous crowd.

For me, it was deja vu. My mind traveled back to the 1960s civil rights movement and the resulting mob violence on the streets of Tampa. The rocks, bottles, gunshots, burning cars, and commercial buildings brought back memories. Several of my officers, never having experienced such violence on this scale, were obviously in awe.

While patrolling, I observed an interesting phenomenon: black residents who were spectators were standing on the street by their homes or on sidewalks throughout their neighborhood, wondering what the hell was happening. Few of them realized the rioters were standing in the dark areas behind them, throwing rocks and bottles over their heads at the police and passing traffic.

It was reminiscent of the 1960s to watch the reaction of young officers under riot conditions, being the target of derogatory outbursts, confronted with the gunshots, fires, catcalls, ducking rocks and bottles. Rioters would run and fade into the darkness of night, into alleyways and other hideouts, or just meld into a crowd of onlookers. This left the officers with no immediate ability to take corrective action or enforcement measures they were conditioned to

THE SPARK AND ENERGY OF RIOTS

take. It caused some of them to become frustrated and lash out at anyone in their path. Their abrupt and rigid manner and approach to people, many of whom were just bystanders, was a symptom of that frustration.

Trying to set an example, I would accompany young officers who were approaching residents and other onlookers to briefly explain what was happening. I told them we would appreciate their cooperation by remaining in their yards, or better yet, for their own and their family's safety, in their homes. This would greatly assist us in making the distinction between spectators and troublemakers. Every individual or group we approached in this manner not only cooperated but expressed their appreciation for the respectful manner with which they were treated.

In one case, while we were explaining the circumstances to residents, a young black lady with a small baby in her arms challenged our authority to ask them to leave the area. I took the time to explain what was happening. I pointed to an empty beer bottle on the ground near her, but before I could finish explaining, another bottle landed close by that was thrown from the darkness of an alleyway. The young mother reached down, picked up both bottles, and said, "You're right. I'm taking my baby home, and these bottles won't be thrown at you again, Officer."

When the rioting waned, we headed back over the Bascule Bridge toward Treasure Island. I was driving, it was very quiet, and a breeze passed through our opened patrol car windows. Crossing over the bridge, the silence was broken when Detective Dave Schilt said, "Ah, good old Treasure Island."

It was a moment for Dave but also a sense of appreciation from the other officers in the car for their positions in our small town. I too could appreciate that this night had just been a glimpse of what I had experienced over the years with the Tampa Police Department.

Unbeknownst to my young colleagues, we had a round-trip ticket to South St. Petersburg as the violence wasn't over. Again, a month after the shooting, when Officer Knight was cleared by the grand jury of any criminal conduct, we were thrust back into the rock-and-bottle festivities. The grand jury stated Knight's actions were taken

153

in self-defense. Not only was Knight cleared criminally, he appealed the department's disciplinary action, a sixty-day suspension without pay; and an arbitrator reversed the city's action, stating that the police department could not or did not produce a policy restricting police officers from placing themselves in the front of a suspect's car.

I doubt that Officer Knight would have suffered a lengthy suspension had the suspect been a white man. Plainly, the race issue had influenced the disciplinary action against him. True, the officer should not have placed himself in jeopardy by standing in the car's path. At the time, he only had minor charges against the suspect, hardly a case for placing himself in harm's way. On the other side of the coin, Knight and Minor were doing their job as police officers. All the rule books and tons of written policies cannot erase the quick decision-making dilemma that cops are thrust into on just about a daily basis.

Training, of course, is a tool that can eliminate tons of Monday morning quarterbacking when these types of incidents occur. Proper hands-on training is the key to drastically reducing the tragic end of such cases. Far too many officers have been crucified, not for unforgivable decisions, but to douse the racial and political heat that often comes with the territory of leadership. Remember the words "If you can't take the heat, get out of the kitchen." Nobody said doing the right thing was always going to be easy. In this case, both the police department's and city's leadership lacked the intestinal fortitude to support their officer. They capitulated under pressure from black community leaders who had no interest in what was "right."

This scenario is no different than Lewis pointing a gun at Knight and Knight shooting in self-defense.

It would have been interesting to see the results of a media conducted poll of black citizens, taken after the riot, to determine their viewpoint on the riots and the Knight vs. Lewis incident. I'd venture a guess that the majority of them would have voiced their disgust with the criminal conduct of those outnumbered radicals in the black community.

The conclusion of an internal affairs investigative report by the St. Petersburg Police Department should have read, "Officer Knight may have made a bad decision by positioning himself in front of the suspect's car, but to claim his actions caused the death of Lewis is wrongheaded. TyRon Lewis's refusal to obey the lawful orders of the police, driving forward toward Officer Knight with sufficient force to knock him onto the hood of his car, is what caused his demise." Case closed.

13

Crowd Control

I had just been promoted to patrol lieutenant and was working the day shift in patrol district 2. I arrived for duty on a Sunday morning and poured myself a cup of coffee. It sure felt different coming to work and not rushing out on the street at the beginning of the shift.

But my ass had no sooner hit the chair at my new desk when the captain called me into his office and said, "Get up to Rowlett Park! That renegade rock band is at it again."

Somewhat surprised at the captain's agitation, I asked, "What the hell are you talking about, Captain?"

Because I hadn't worked district two in several years, I didn't know that a rock group had been taking over the park on Sunday mornings and pissing off those still sleeping. Many people do enjoy sleeping late on Sundays.

As I prepared to depart for the park located at the extreme northern end of the city, the captain stated, "You should know the mayor has received numerous complaints and made it clear last week that the very next time the band started up again, the park would be closed, but you make your own decision."

Oh yeah, I thought, *I'll certainly go against the mayor*. En route to the park, I ordered the north-end squad to meet me there.

About five or six blocks from the park, I could hear the band. Entering the park, I observed a very large crowd of young people at the makeshift stage, rocking back and forth to the band's loud and raucous music. I proceeded over a hill and met with about two dozen officers and a corporal who was the acting sergeant that day. We didn't expect to scare too many people, considering we had a crowd that was about five hundred strong. With just two dozen officers, we merely wanted to surprise them.

After discussing a plan with the corporal, we were ready for action. Hugging the hill on the crowd's blindside, I lined up officers on both sides of my cruiser at double arm's length. The line of officers extended the entire length of the hill. I gave the order, and we proceeded over the hill, with the siren blaring and emergency lights flashing. The park was cleared within five minutes, and only two or three arrests were necessary.

*

It was the Tampa Bay Buccaneers' second year in football, and they were playing the last game of the season at home. The week before in New Orleans, they had won their first game ever against the Saints. This week they were playing the St. Louis Cardinals and Tampa Stadium was packed.

When the Bucs ran out onto the field to start the game, it was pandemonium. The players trotted around the field, giving the victory sign and thumbs up. The fans went nuts. I was the selective enforcement unit (SEU) captain, and all four of my squads were assigned traffic control at key intersections on the approach to the stadium before and after the game.

With the exception of my officers and me, all other officers were working the stadium event in an off-duty capacity and were being paid directly by the football stadium. In addition to Tampa police officers, there were Hillsborough County deputies and Florida Highway Patrol troopers working it as well.

The Bucs scored first and held the lead throughout the game. Just moments before the end of the game, it became apparent the Bucs were going to win their first home game ever.

During these stadium events, I was stationed in the stadium tower before the games, watching the incoming crowd of fans and again after the game was over and the fans began their exit. From the tower I had a panoramic view of all traffic arteries surrounding the stadium. I maintained radio communications with my officers stationed at their key traffic control intersections, keeping them informed of traffic flow and coordinated outbound traffic from the stadium.

This particular crowd was really wound up. Even before the end of the game, some were intent on climbing over the spectator's retaining wall onto the field. I discussed the crowd control situation with the major in charge. I visualized what we could expect when the game ended. I recommended keeping my four squads in the stadium to control the crowd. I anticipated a swarm of people spilling onto the field once the game ended. In the end, we decided the four SEU squads would maintain their original assignment of traffic control.

With just moments until the end of the game, the fans were on their feet, pressed against the retaining wall. When the game clock hit ten seconds with the Bucs winning, the fans began counting, "Ten, nine, eight, seven . . ." At zero, there was no stopping them. From the tower, it looked like a huge swarm of bees pouring onto the field.

The goalposts were the first casualties. When they came down, one man was trapped and ended up with a broken leg. The crowd was out of control, sixty thousand people, seemingly all on a mission to wreck the field. One field-goal net was pulled down, and a police sergeant was trapped in it. He was dragged halfway down the field before several fans could get him out. Seats were ripped out of the stands. Even sod on the field was being taken as souvenirs. Very little could be done to control the out-of-control fans. Several more hours of traffic control at key intersections was required to deal with the drunk celebrating fans leaving the stadium, placing police officers in greater danger of injury or worse.

In certain large gatherings, crowds take on a personality of their own. It seems as if people morph into a collection of morons. Gatherings can start out as legitimate sports and music events but then it happens—the drug use, alcohol consumption, spectators start throwing bottles, or kicking out windows when exiting. Such misconduct is contagious and encourages others to follow suit.

Usually, additional police reinforcements are required to disperse a crowd, resulting in arrests and in some cases, use of tear gas.

*

Demonstrators and protest marchers can morph into a violent huge animal much more quickly than even sports and entertainment crowds. So-called peaceful demonstrations often start out with mostly good people that have the best intentions; but frequently mixed in are those few radicals and troublemakers whose intentions are adverse to folks peacefully marching or demonstrating.

Labor strikes start out relatively free of violent or destructive acts, but when strike issues are not readily resolved and time drags on with no salary coming in and bills mounting up, strikers become anxious and retaliatory. Labor strikes can quickly evolve into violence. The longer the strike, the uglier it can get.

In the early to mid-1960s, there was a telephone workers strike. Tempers were short, and what may have been tolerable or insignificant early on in the strike became magnified; short fuses resulted in violence and destruction of company property.

Large phone line trunks were being chopped in half all over the city. Work crews, many of them phone company supervisors or managers, diligently repaired the vandalized underground phone line trunks. This only exacerbated the situation, and the police had to deploy units to protect the workers, at least to make frequent checks on the working crews. The strikers became so desperate and angry they planned to cut a number of critical phone line trunks accessing hospitals and other emergency facilities. In addition, problems progressed to the point that several strikers prepared to set up a rooftop sniper post.

I remember stopping a traffic violator on West Hillsborough Avenue one afternoon as he pulled into a shopping center. I approached the car; but before I could say anything, the driver got out, slammed the door shut, and began yelling, almost out of control but not specifically threatening me. I immediately thought, *He's a telephone worker,* and he was. In essence, he was just totally frustrated about overdue bills, and pulling him over was the final straw.

The first thing I said was "I'm not going to give you a ticket." I thought, this guy doesn't need this now. The violation was not reckless, so I just wrote it up as a warning. I did say, "You need to settle down before driving off." We talked a few moments, he extended his hand, we shook, and both departed.

Another strike in the early 1980s involved truckers. Hooker's Point, an industrial park, is on a peninsula extending south into Hillsborough Bay. Twentieth Street south takes you right down into Hooker's Point. The truckers had set up their strike team on Twentieth Street at a point just north of the bend in the road that leads to Hooker's Point. While there were a few homes on the east side of the street, the west side of Twentieth Street was mostly open fields. With each passing day, more and more trucks were parked along the west side of Twentieth Street. Extending north, the parked trucks began to interfere with traffic.

When this type of strike lingers, strikers become frustrated and angry and begin to think of nasty little things to do to nonunion workers filling in during the strike. When the union truckers started throwing large nails in the roadway, we decided it was time to act. Up until that time, only a few officers and several Hillsborough County deputies were at the strike area.

I was the patrol district 2 division commander. I teamed up with a major, my counterpart representing the Hillsborough County Sheriff's Office, and we headed out to the strike area to educate the strikers. The sheriff's major, though very competent and intelligent, carried himself with the attitude "I'm the best there is in this position." I was looking forward to observing the sheriff's major communicating across educational, economic, and regional lines with the strikers. As we approached, my counterpart took the first crack at communicating with them.

Approaching the trucker who was apparently the leader of the pack, the major started in with a string of technical issues related to the law. It was comical to observe the facial expressions of the lead trucker and those standing beside and behind him. Each time the major stopped, anticipating a reaction or response from the leader, all he got was "Huh?"

Frustrated, after several attempts to communicate with the trucker, the major looked over at me and said, "You tell them."

I did. Without hesitation, I stepped up the truckers' fearless leader and said in a loud, clear tone, "Get these fucking trucks out of here, or we start impounding them and putting your asses in jail."

Half the strikers then headed for their trucks, but several others wanted to cry on my shoulder about tire punctures they would get from the nails *they* dumped in the roadway. I countered with, "Tough shit, you put them there. Now move these trucks, or they will be impounded."

These guys thought they had been so smart dumping nails in the road. They purposely bent them in a fashion so that the spiked ends would stick straight up. As the trucks pulled out, I heard a few pops, and bent nails began flying behind the moving trucks. Within a few minutes, though, the trucks were gone. See how easy it is when you know how to communicate?

*

Rock-music shows back in the 1970s had a twisted life of their own. Trying to enforce laws regarding unlawful drug use in a crowd of thousands of people was nearly impossible. The ultimate frustrating conclusion was people smoking, snorting, and injecting their dope; the risk of officer injury was reason enough to simply control usage as much as possible, given the sheer amount of drugs coming into the stadium.

Inevitably there was a spectator or two needing emergency medical attention during the show. It was the responsibility of the police to forge through the crowd creating an access line for paramedics. Once the police penetrated the crowd, there were those who wanted to rebel, believing we were there to arrest people.

One particular concert is seared into my memory. It was June 3, 1977, when a famous rock band came to Tampa Stadium. I viewed the interior of the stadium and the surrounding traffic arteries from the tower. Approximately thirty thousand people crammed onto the field before dark. The stage was huge, at that time the biggest I'd ever seen. It had to be three to four stories high and was erected at the south end of the football field.

A retaining wall had been constructed to restrict spectators from accessing the stage area. Made of thick four-by-eight-foot sheets of plywood framed in angle iron extending beyond the ends of the stage from one side of the stadium to the other, it was supported by steel posts every few feet on the secure side of the wall. Anyone intent on climbing over the wall would have to jump up to grab the top of it. Each end of the wall was a reinforced plywood door to access the field, if necessary. During the show, officers were assigned behind the wall.

Fans with tickets entered the stadium through constructed cattle chutes and had to submit to a search for drugs and alcohol before gaining admittance. All drugs and containers or bottles of alcohol were seized. In cases involving serious amounts of hard drugs, arrests were made. Even with all this security, fans managed to smuggle in plenty of drugs and booze. Once ticket sales ended, the outer gates surrounding the exterior of the stadium were locked to prevent people from sneaking in or actually crashing the gates.

Within a few moments after the show started, we experienced a thunderstorm with serious lightning. People on the field crammed in under the stadium, but about half of them wouldn't fit and remained on the field. The spectator stands were not used for rock shows.

What happened next was the catalyst for a riot. The musicians, fearful of performing during a lightning storm, panicked and fled the stadium in their limos. They subsequently told the media that the Tampa police ran them out of the stadium when in fact a group of us tried desperately to convince them that once the storm was over, there would be no danger of lightning. But it all fell on deaf ears, and they sped off with car doors still swinging open. They knew very well what would happen when the fans realized they were not coming back out on the stage. They simply didn't care.

Again, I had the dilemma of either leaving my officers on traffic posts for the exiting fans or bringing them into the stadium because we were going to have a very large and angry mob of fans to deal with. I made the decision to bring all four squads, about forty officers, into the stadium. The stadium lights were shut off to give us time to organize and maneuver into strategic positions around the stadium.

162

To control or repel the crowd on the other side of the retaining wall, several squads of reinforced officers, including me, were already behind it. When the crowd realized the band members had fled, as I had predicted, all hell broke loose.

We timed our entry onto the field with the working stadium crews who were opening all the gates. We had to give the crews time to get around to all the gates before pushing the crowd back, otherwise people would have been crushed. We could already hear fans, those closest to the stage area, yelling for help. Liquor bottles were flying in every direction. In an attempt to get on the stage, fans began trying to climb over the wall. They would jump and grab the top of the plywood, and officers would have no choice but to whack their fingers with their nightsticks. But in several places, overzealous fans actually breached the wall. Our nightsticks had a good workout that night.

We opened the end doors on the retaining wall, entered the field, and faced the mob. Officers pushed back in a line formation, and most fans scattered. I spotted a fan in a wheelchair stuck in the mud on the field. He was trying to make it to the wall door but liquor bottles were being thrown from every direction. I ran to him, placed my helmet over his head, and with the help of someone else—an officer or spectator, to this day I'm not sure who—we managed to get him to safety.

One officer was actually overpowered, receiving minor injuries, and several rioters managed to steal his gun and badge. Within moments, however, two spectators approached the police officers on the field with their hands in the air, carrying the officer's gun and badge. They had witnessed what had happened and apparently being very capable young men, retrieved them from the suspects.

By now, the field was almost cleared but the diehards had gotten into the spectator stands and were throwing bottles at us. The lights were turned back on, lighting up the stadium. Officers were just about ready to charge the stands and start grabbing the bastards when I ordered them not to. I lined officers up back-to-back in two rows, each row facing one of the two main spectator stands on the east and west sides of the stadium. I grabbed a bullhorn from a sergeant and told the officers to wait; the jerks would be running out of bottles in a minute. The distance between the diehards throwing the bottles and the lines of officers offered plenty of time to dodge the bottles. In fact, another commander and I actually caught some thrown bottles with our bullhorns.

Within a few minutes, our friends indeed ran out of bottles. Looking around the stadium, they realized they were trapped. For just a brief moment there was silence. Officers looked up at the rioters who were looking back down at us. The officers then looked over at me with a gleam in their eyes, and a voice came from the line: "Now, Captain Joe—now?"

I only hesitated long enough to suppress a laugh and said, "Yes. Now go get them!" At this point, the rioters had no avenue of escape, and we corralled them all.

There were numerous injuries as a result of this civil disobedience. Unfortunately, many of the injured spectators played no part in the violence. Because most of the young fans were barefoot or just wearing flip-flops or sandals, many left the stadium limping and nursing lacerated feet from broken glass.

It's always just a small percentage of people who create the problem. But in this case, that was several thousand violent fans. About thirty-five officers were injured, some requiring medical treatment. The city refused to allow any more rock concerts after this one.

*

Waterborne sports should be restricted to skilled boaters, divers, swimmers, and skiers. Any event involving a great number of people is risky. Unskilled contestants don't comprehend any danger beyond drowning. Most people who can swim are overconfident and oblivious to any other dangers. How many times have you witnessed young children without life jackets while in a boat with Mom and Dad? How many boaters venture out miles from shore without a fire extinguisher or first aid kit? How many people aren't aware of bad weather predictions when they go out on the water or just choose to ignore them, thinking they can ride out a storm?

In the early 1980s, the City of Tampa, along with some private enterprises, sponsored a river raft race on the Hillsborough River. It was a one-day event, beginning miles upriver from downtown Tampa. The launching site was almost a disaster before the race started.

An unspecified number of contestants were drunk before the event began, and it wasn't even noon yet. Rafts were jammed in the water so tightly, most were pressing up against each other. Fights broke out and people fired water-filled balloons both from rafts and from the shoreline as the rafts traveled downstream.

One officer on marine patrol was struck in the head by a water balloon, causing him to fall to the deck, which resulted in a head injury. A woman had fallen off a raft and slid below the surface. Because once underwater there wasn't a sufficient open area to surface, she drowned.

The following year, the second annual raft race resulted in more injuries, and another person almost drowned.

When we approached the third annual raft race, as the deputy police chief, I recommended in writing that it be cancelled. The event was too dangerous, and the risk of loss of life was too great. I emphasized that safety should take priority over any financial motives to sponsor the race.

My caveat, however, was ignored—but eventually the raft races were discontinued. Why does it always take tragedy to wake people up? This event was a recipe for disaster.

*

While labor strikes, demonstrations, sporting events, music festivals, and rock shows are reasonably confined to a fixed controllable area, parades are always especially hectic. Pedestrians morph into spectators ranging in age from kids in the arms of their parents to seniors in wheelchairs.

Parades require officers stretched out for miles along the parade route, and if additional police assistance is required, response time is delayed. Traffic control is commensurate and blended in with crowd control. In many cases, more officers are needed for parades than for most other events.

Tampa's Gasparilla pirate parade and celebration goes back to the early 1900s. For the police, there were no days off on Gasparilla

Day. All officers, including detectives and administrative personnel, worked in uniform. The main daytime parade went through downtown Tampa while the night parade took place Saturday night in Ybor City on Broadway, Seventh Avenue. It generally coincided with the Florida State Fair, which only increased the crowds on the day of the Gasparilla parade.

My first Gasparilla parade assignment was traffic control at one of the busiest intersections in the city: Hillsborough and Florida avenues. Both are state roadways and main traffic arteries in and out of downtown Tampa. The interstate highway system did not exist in Tampa at that time.

The sergeant dropped me off at about 9:00 AM. By 10:00 AM, the incoming traffic was backing up from the north, east, and west. I was in the intersection and directed traffic right up to the time the parade started at 1:00 PM.

After the parade ended, there was a mass exodus; and I was back in the intersection, directing traffic, which at one point, was backed up in the northbound lanes of Florida Avenue at least a mile from my traffic post.

At 7:00 PM, my sergeant drove by and said, "Get in."

I responded, "But traffic is still backed up."

"Forget it," the sergeant said. "Get in. Traffic is going to be like this until midnight, but at least the downtown area is now cleared of traffic." There were no further arguments from me.

On parade day, parking was always a nightmare in residential neighborhoods—driveways were blocked, streets were sometimes impassible, and sightseers parked in residents' front yards. In many cases, officers were on their own when trouble with spectators occurred or with other problems requiring immediate police attention.

The Gasparilla parade draws many thousands of spectators. During a night parade, I was posted at East Broadway and Fourteenth Street in Ybor City. The closest help I had were two other officers posted a block away in each direction along the parade route, but we had no portable radio communications back then.

Though it was already dark when the parade started, the area was well illuminated. You have to appreciate the problem with noise, though, in addition to loud passing bands and spectators yelling. Tampa's businessmen were all dressed up as pirates and were constantly firing blanks from their revolvers. Just behind me, on the northeast corner of the intersection, was a gas station.

At the peak of the parade, one enterprising thug decided to rob the gas station. There was only one attendant on duty. With all the pirates firing off their blanks, I was not immediately aware that actual shots were being fired. A spectator directly across the street facing me could see the robbery going on and alerted me with arm gestures and by pointing.

When I turned around, the gas station attendant was standing just outside the office on the sidewalk facing north and was holding a pistol. I immediately spotted someone just north of the attendant lying on the ground. I recognized the attendant and blew my whistle while running to his aid.

It seems the robber had approached the attendant in a threatening manner with a crowbar in hand. The attendant had chased the robber out of the station and up Fourteenth Street, firing a shot. This missed the suspect entirely, but struck a bystander in the leg, who then fell to the sidewalk just south of Eighth Avenue. Considering all the excitement of the parade, the huge crowd and the robbery, I was relieved that no one else had been shot.

During one parade, I barely escaped serious injury. I was assigned to crowd and traffic control on Kennedy Boulevard and Plant Avenue. The parade floats, bands, and horse brigades had to turn onto Kennedy Boulevard from Plant Avenue. The turn was tight for some floats, and it was a constant problem keeping the spectators back from the road and away from the turning floats.

At one point, I had turned my back on the parade to monitor the spectators when someone screamed nearby. I looked over my shoulder just in time to see the extra-large-sized ass of a Clydesdale horse slipping and falling. That big ass was bearing down on me, but if the good Lord gave me nothing else, he gave me speed. I felt the breeze as the big reddish brown ass hit the pavement inches from my scrawny little white ass. That was a scare I would have just as soon avoided.

14

Animal Antics

The funny stories about police encounters with animals are endless. Dogs, cats, bulls, cows, alligators, horses, snakes, giant pet lizards, rodents, ducks, and the bat—err—beat goes on.

On a hot summer day in Tampa, my partner Bill Henley drove into a weeded field just south of Adamo Drive in the East Tampa area of the city, near the East Tampa Bay shoreline. It was only 10:00 AM, and already we had four reports to write: three residential burglaries and a minor traffic accident. Bill turned down the dry, dusty dirt road, stopping about thirty yards from the end track of a railroad service port used for repairing train locomotives. We threw open the cruiser doors to savor the breeze coming off the bay, and we began writing. Occasionally, a call in our patrol zone went out over the police radio; but Bill looked over at me, and I blurted out, "No. Let's stay out of service and catch up on these reports. We have two hours of report writing to do, and zone 5 can handle this call. They've had only one call in their zone since we started."

After coming off a call, patrol units are supposed to go 10-8 (back in service) immediately and be available to respond to calls while sitting somewhere writing reports. But everyone stayed out of service when bogged down with three or four reports. Some officers really took advantage and never came back in service until they had finished all their reports.

After about thirty minutes of sweating, writing reports, and listening to cars roaring along Adamo Drive, I heard a strange sound. Bill looked up, so I knew he heard it too. An animal was whining or crying. The field we were parked in was flat with thinned-out, foot-high weeds, so we should have been able to see an animal in any direction that was close enough to hear.

I said, "It's coming from that railroad service port."

As we walked toward the port, we could hear a distinct cry that sounded like a puppy. We entered the port area and observed a cement pit filled with water, sludge, and oil. The top waterline was about six feet below ground level. We were surprised to see a small dog, no more than twelve pounds, covered with black oil. He was submerged up to his neck, with his front paws clinging to a floating piece of wood, struggling to keep his head up. He looked up at us with pleading eyes. We quickly scanned the area and found a piece of rope. After several attempts, we managed to loop it around the pup's neck and started to gently pull him over to the edge of the pit, only to have him slip out and under the oil slick.

We were desperate and thought we'd lost him. But he managed to bob back up, still looking at us with those pleading eyes.

Finally, after several more attempts, we got the rope around his neck again. Bill yelled, "We got him!" This time we got him up on the deck, and he expressed his appreciation by shaking the water and oil off his body and onto my uniform. I swear, he barked twice as he ran off, like saying, "Thanks and good-bye!" The rest of the shift somehow seemed easier after that.

*

Thoughts of Sassy, our first K-9, bring back funny memories of when she first started on the job.

The Hillsborough County Sheriff's Department K-9 Unit was very helpful in the initial training of the dog and her handler. During one training scenario, two deputies wearing padded protective sleeves were hiding behind separate bushes but within arm's length of each other. Sassy found one deputy, alerted her handler by barking, and while keeping her eyes on him, the other deputy reached out from his hiding place and slapped her on the rump with the sleeve.

Sassy turned her attention from the first deputy to the one that slapped her and continued barking. Then the first deputy leaned over from behind his bush and slapped her on the rump. Sassy again turned her attention, continued barking and got slapped yet again. After about six alternating slaps on the rump, she stopped barking, walked over, and sat down alongside her handler. Now facing the two deputies simultaneously, she began barking at them both.

*

One night, Officer Elliot, Sassy's handler, received a burglary-in-progress call at a public school. Almost invariably, the burglars are long gone when the police arrive on these calls.

In this case, when the K-9 unit rolled up to a side entrance close to the rear of the school building, Officer Elliot observed two white males exit the door. He yelled for them to stop and raise their hands. One did, but the other one ran. The K-9 patrol car was not yet equipped with automatic door or window openers. The officer reached around and opened the rear door and yelled for Sassy to get him.

The suspect who complied with the officer's command had his hands up over his head and was leaning against his own car. Expecting Sassy to react to her training and chase after the suspect who ran, Officer Elliot approached the surrendered suspect to handcuff him. But Sassy hadn't seen the suspect who ran, only the one leaning against the car, so she ran by the officer, throwing her full weight against the suspect. Hind legs on the ground, her front legs pressed against the suspect's chest, she showed him her beautiful big white teeth accompanied by a very determined growl.

The officer, realizing this, changed direction and pursued the fleeing suspect on foot. Eventually returning empty handed, he observed that Sassy hadn't moved. She was still growling and displaying her beautiful large white teeth.

The suspect, who hadn't moved, said to the officer with tears in his eyes, "Officer, please get your dog."

*

One hot summer day, Officer D. J. Halligan and I were working the day shift in Sulfur Springs. We received a call and responded to a house on East Yukon Avenue. The homeowner complained about an animal in the house.

Upon arrival, we approached the small wooden frame shotgun house. These older homes, built between the 1920s and 1930s, are called shotgun houses because of their layout. Entering the front door, you're in the living room and can see straight through to the back door. A bullet shot from a gun at the front door could easily sail right out the back door.

A lady in her fifties greeted us with her southern drawl. "He's back. You said you would take care of him, but he's back."

I asked, "Who's back, lady?"

She responded, "That ugly possum. The officers that were here last week said they would get rid of him, and now he's back!"

She led us to the kitchen which bordered the closed-in back porch. On the same wall as the door leading to the back porch was a counter with a line of large deep drawers used for storing flour and bread products. She pointed to one of the drawers and said, "He's in that one."

D. J. opened the drawer and was met with a mouthful of the ugliest teeth in the world. The possum lunged at him, snarling, and dripping with saliva. We both jumped back. D. J. yelled, "Yikes!" and kicked the drawer shut.

I asked, "How the hell did he get in the drawer?"

The lady explained that when her husband installed the drawers, he didn't seal up the bottom of the partition, which originally was the back wall of the kitchen. This gave our friend access from a two-foot crawl space under the house. I asked her how the first officer caught him. She said he just grabbed him around the neck and carried him out—after being bitten on the hand.

I told D. J. we definitely needed a burlap sack or a box of some sort to capture the little twerp. We had no desire to end up being bitten by this ugly moocher. The old lady mumbled something in her southern drawl, like "damn animals" and walked off into the backyard. She returned with an old Texaco cardboard box blotched with motor oil stains.

We decided D. J. would place the box over the closed drawer, at the same time I would pull it open with the handle of a broom, then turn the broom around and use the whisk end to scoop the possum into the box. Unbelievably, we managed to do just that.

The fun part was trying to keep him in the closed box and not be bitten in the process. D. J. assured the lady we'd make sure Homer the Horrible, as we affectionately named him, wouldn't be back.

Back in the cruiser, we heard a neighbor laugh and yell, "Skin 'im out. It's good eatin'!"

I yelled back, "No thanks. I'll stick with hamburgers."

Our friend was not a happy camper. I had to sit in the backseat and hold the box close by placing my foot on it because he was definitely trying to make the great escape. I told D. J. that if this little bastard got out of the box, there would be bullet holes in the cruiser.

I asked D. J. how we were going to dispose of our friend, and he answered by heading for an old abandoned airfield just north of the lady's house. He wanted to have some target practice on the possum, but I didn't feel the same way.

When we arrived at the field, D. J. dumped the animal on the ground and was getting ready to shoot him as he ran away. But the poor guy couldn't run. He only had three working legs. The right hind leg was very tiny, shriveled up, and drawn up close to his buttocks. He was scared and attempted to hobble away from us as quickly as he could.

I looked at D. J. His jaw dropped open, his hand falling off his gun handle and down to his side. I know he felt sorry for the crippled possum and couldn't shoot him. He shifted his eyes from the possum over to me and said, "Err, you shoot first."

My response was "Not me."

We climbed back in the cruiser and headed north as the possum headed south in the direction of the lady's house. We agreed to remember the lady's address in case we received another call and make sure we were busy with some other problem.

I knew I wouldn't have shot at that possum. As a young boy, I found my father's old BB gun in the attic and took it out in the backyard when no one else was home. I shot a small bird, a robin redbreast, perched on a tree limb. It fell to the ground, dead. I was stunned because I just wasn't smart enough to realize the BB would kill the bird. I have never killed an animal for sport, and I never could.

*

Whoever said, "See you later, alligator," was smart. A single encounter with an angry alligator and you will gain a warehouse full of respect for them and want to leave the scene as soon as possible. If I didn't know better, I would have thought Florida was another word for alligator. Everywhere you go, there they are.

During my first few years in Florida, I saw gators in zoos or in roadside souvenir shops as pocketbooks and shoes. But my first introduction to a wild one occurred as I was swimming in a lake. Lake Ralston was just outside the city limits of Tampa and was a privately operated swimming facility with a snack bar, picnic tables, rafts, diving platforms, and barbeque pits.

One evening after closing, we were allowed to stay late because the owner liked GIs. I was halfway out in the middle of the lake swimming back toward shore. Except for the distant voices of my friends on the beach, it was very quiet and serene. Suddenly I sensed someone or something close by. Looking back, I spotted a ripple about twenty-five feet directly behind me. I stopped swimming for a moment and spotted an alligator with his two little eyes focused on me. Once closer to shore I stood up and the gator turned around and his tail broke the surface. I was quite surprised to see that he had to be about five or six feet long.

Everywhere I went, fishing or swimming, there were gators. I even hooked one on a bass plug fishing with my friend in the Little

Manatee River. Any creek, pond, or storm-sewer pipe will host alligators. I don't care if it is twenty-five feet from a school yard, a supermarket in a strip mall, or a pond in a public park—it's got gators.

While on patrol one day, I was sent to the intersection of Dale Mabry and Henderson Boulevard on a report of a merchant sighting a small alligator walking along the sidewalk. It was the rainy season, and I arrived at the scene just as a downpour stopped. The water in the intersection was two or three feet deep.

Gators routinely access the storm-sewer drainage system and travel anywhere they want to. This gator appeared to be about three feet long. Small, right? This little guy was prancing up and down in front of storefronts as if he was shopping. I approached Smiley with nightstick in hand, not giving much thought to any problem I would encounter with such a small gator.

When I tried to corner him, he took it very personally and gave me a view of all his teeth. He was so fast it seemed like this twerp could run in both directions at the same time. When I became desperate to corner him, I poked my nightstick at him; again, he took offense and this time grabbed the end of it. You would think a grown man could have merely jerked the stick out of his ugly mouth, but this gator had a set of jaws like Dad's workshop vise. No way was this guy going to surrender the nightstick. I pulled with both hands, but no dice.

Finally, another patrol unit arrived. It was a traffic officer who I learned later was an experienced alligator handler. He stepped up, grabbed the gator, threw it in the backseat of his cruiser, and left. My nightstick did not survive, it was dead at the scene, and so I threw it away.

*

One afternoon when I was patrol sergeant, in the August heat of ninety-three plus degrees, I heard one of my patrol officers dispatched to Fort Homer Hesterly on Howard Avenue in reference to a large alligator in the front-screened porch of the military caretaker's living quarters. When I arrived and approached the house, I asked my officer, "Whatcha got?"

He pointed to the front porch screen door. I walked over, opened it, and one really pissed off ten-foot alligator swung around to face me standing in the doorway. This guy had no desire to get acquainted with me, and the feeling was mutual. We called animal control and stood by.

How did the gator get in the screened porch? Well, there are pranks and then there are pranks. The caretaker, a sergeant, was transferred temporarily to another military site, but his wife remained. The night before he was to depart, they had a small party; and his buddies, drunk, dumped the critter in the porch as a joke, not thinking any more about it. After several days in the heat and sun, this gator, without water, was not happy.

The animal-control men knew their business. When they arrived and scrutinized the scene, they knew they had their hands full. In fact, while wrangling this gator, one of them was bitten on the leg, requiring stitches. The gator was so furious at one point it almost got free of the restraints; and we thought we might have to destroy it, but fortunately, the handlers were ultimately successful in restraining it.

*

I was a patrol lieutenant in the early 1970s. The lieutenants were field commanders and acted as the shift commander when the captain was off or otherwise not available. Though administrative paperwork occupied much of a lieutenant's workday, I always made time to get out on the street.

I remember one busy weekend night responding from one hot call to another. My intent was not to take over or take charge of a situation unless it was urgent, but to determine if the sergeant and/or officers needed anything from me. If not, I would leave.

This particular night, I overheard a unit get a call of an alligator in a resident's backyard bordering the Hillsborough River. It apparently slipped in under a chain-link fence and was after a dog that was tied up.

After responding to several other calls, I kept hearing conversation over the radio about getting the alligator to the river. I decided to drive by and get a bird's-eye view of the situation.

This gator had to be at least ten feet long. I don't know how they did it, but the officers had a rope around its neck and were walking it down the middle of the street toward the river. When the gator stopped walking, the officers would wait until it decided to walk again. I grabbed the rope from the officer and pulled the gator. As long as you pulled on the rope, he would walk. The riverbank was about a block away.

Arriving at the riverbank, the gator walked to the seawall and stopped with his head hanging right over the river.

I said, "We need to get the rope off his neck."

One officer reached in his pocket and handed me a pocketknife. How much more cooperation could you ask from one of your fellow officers?

After taking the knife, I said, "Thanks."

The officer smiled and said, "You're welcome."

I reached over, staying as far from the gator as possible, almost in a kneeling position. I kept both feet on the ground for a fast retreat if my friend decided to get aggressive, but he remained in the same position with his head hanging over the seawall. I stretched out as far as I could without losing my balance and slid the knife under the rope, cut it, and just like it was what he was waiting for, the gator then slipped into the water and disappeared; and so did we.

*

On one midnight shift, at about 4:00 AM, several patrol units were dispatched to handle a young bull running loose in the street adjacent to the dog racetrack in Sulfur Springs.

We located our guy, munching on weeds along the racetrack fence line on Bird Street, between Florida and Nebraska avenues, but he took off running toward Florida Avenue. The term *young* doesn't always equate with *small size*. This guy was a biiiig bull. When he spotted us, he ran like a seasoned burglar with no intention of being caught. As he turned southbound on Florida Avenue, things got interesting.

The bull was running down the middle of the street with four police cruisers in pursuit, all with overhead lights on, just as a house was being towed north on Florida Avenue by a house-moving team. The bull ran around the house with all four cruisers paired off on either side of the house. The house-moving team threw us a good length of rope with a laughing yell of "good luck!"

By now, our young friend was running along the muddy bank of the Hillsborough River, the patrol units closing in behind him. I could see Officer D. J. Halligan in one cruiser, laughing and ordering his rookie to do something. Then his passenger side door opened and while the cruiser was moving, the rookie bailed out and landed facedown, flat like a pancake in the mud. D. J. laughed and slowed down, allowing the rest of us to pull ahead. The bull finally stopped running, and we surrounded him on foot.

The officer with the rope lassoed him, and as he tried to wrap the rope around a tree, the bull decided to chase him. The officer was running in a circle around the tree with the bull right on his ass. By now, D. J. wasn't the only one laughing. Once the rope ran out, the bull stopped, as did the officer who just let go of the rope. They were both exhausted. Then the rookie caught up on foot, covered from head to toe in mud. At that point, everybody was laughing. I even think I saw a smirk on the bull's face. Nah.

*

Lizards never smile. At least alligators sometimes appear to grin. I'm positive that in some ancient language, *iguana* meant "sourpuss." Why anyone would want one as a pet is beyond me. Definitions of *pet*: "darling," "model," "love," "dear," "beloved"—all describe cute little animals. But if you include iguanas, then you need to expand the definition to "homely," "uncaring," and "don't you touch me, you human pig."

When one hears a call over the police radio about the caller needing help recapturing her pet iguana, you immediately wonder just what an officer can do that the pet owner can't.

Anyway, this pet owner called the police because her iguana was loose in the yard. I was close by, and so I responded. D. J. still had his rookie, who seemed squeamish beyond the norm. They pulled into the yard right behind me, and I observed the rookie jump out of the cruiser, put his hat on, and hustle around the corner of the house toward the backyard to help the lady find her iguana.

D. J. was slow in getting out and stopped to say something to me when we both heard a shriek. Thinking it was a female voice, we both started around the side of the house. From there, we observed the rookie running down the driveway toward the street, his hat sailing off into the yard. Close behind was a king-sized lizard that appeared to be in pursuit of our rookie. This modern-day dinosaur had to be three feet tall at the head and six or seven feet long. His mouth was wide open, and he was gaining on the rookie who kept running until he was out of sight.

D. J. and I had seen these creatures before and knew they were relatively harmless despite their primitive, menacing appearance. We simultaneously grabbed for the long sweeping tail and couldn't help laughing almost to the point of falling over.

Once we secured Dino, we found the rookie at a phone booth. There was no way was he going back to that house. Needless to say, he never did make probation.

*

One very slow and quiet midnight shift, my partner, Braveheart* was driving. He was somewhat of an enigma, who mumbled when he spoke. I was nodding off in the passenger (shotgun) seat. Considering I held two other jobs, auto mechanic and housepainter and didn't get more than four or five hours of sleep during the day, nodding off was not an unusual occurrence on a slow midnight shift.

Braveheart turned off Westshore Boulevard and headed east on Kennedy Boulevard. When I momentarily looked up, sleepy eyed, I recognized an all-night restaurant called the Waffle House.

I dozed off again and was jolted awake by a loud bloodcurdling scream. I looked up to see the driver's seat empty, the door wide open, and the cruiser still moving slowly along Kennedy Boulevard. Baffled, I looked around and spotted my partner about a half block behind the cruiser, just standing in the middle of the road looking at me, the cruiser moving farther away.

Slamming on the brakes, I looked back at Braveheart, suddenly realizing why he had bailed out. I was staring right at a very large hairy spider within inches of my face, crawling along a large dripping spider web it had just constructed. It extended from one side of the interior to the other on the top of the front seat. I reacted quickly by snatching my new seatmate and flinging him out the driver's side door onto the street.

I pulled into a gas station and used wet paper towels to clean the car seat. When Braveheart settled in the shotgun seat because it was my turn to drive, I asked him what I could expect from him if we had to tangle with any six-foot hairy Homo sapiens? The only response I got were mumbles.

Fortunately, we didn't ride as partners long enough for me to find out. I didn't have much faith in a partner who would bail out of a cruiser while it carried me, napping, down the road just because he didn't like spiders.

*

You really had to know a guy named Art Ramalia to appreciate his exploits. One day, Art, a young patrol officer from my hometown of Brooklyn, New York, received a call to a home on Davis Islands, bordering the southern end of downtown Tampa. The police dispatcher informed him of a large cheetah lying on the front lawn of a house. Art didn't acknowledge the call at first, but then stated very slowly, "Ten-four, and what is it you would like me to do when I get there?"

The dispatcher not having much success in masking her laughter, stated, "Whatever you determine needs to be done." When humorous conversation was heard over the police radio, other patrol units not involved in the call would rapidly click their radio microphones.

In a few moments, Art called the police dispatcher and said, "Okay, there is a large cheetah lying on the front lawn, I'm sitting in my cruiser, he's looking at me, I'm looking at him, he's not moving and neither am I." Click, click, click was heard over the police radio.

Within moments, a station wagon pulled up, the car door opened, and the cheetah ran over and jumped in. The pet owner explained to Art that they had just moved out of the house, were en route to their new one, and realized their pet cheetah was not with them. Art advised the dispatcher, "The cheetah is gone and so am I." Click, click, click . . .

*

Working the midnight shift, there were times when only one officer was assigned to cover all three downtown walking beats. Using a three-wheeled motorcycle, an officer could easily patrol the entire downtown area.

One midnight shift on this assignment, I left the station and proceeded south on Tampa Street toward downtown, turned west, and traveled southbound on Ashley Drive. Approaching the heart of downtown along the east bank of the Hillsborough River, I turned onto what had been a large animal-feed supply building before a raging fire had totally destroyed it. The odor of animal feed still lingered, even after months had passed since the fire.

I stopped within several feet of the riverbank, dismounted the motorcycle, turned the volume up on the police radio, then walked to the river's edge. It was a very quiet night. The night was still with not a hint of a breeze. The river looked like a dark mirror. Tampa University was directly across the river on the west bank. Reflections of the exterior lighting from the university spiked across the surface of the river giving the appearance of large icicles stretching from the west to the east bank.

I stood there savoring the peace and quiet, thinking about how in just seconds all hell could break loose and I'd be racing to a call somewhere downtown. Standing there, a startling sensation came over me, a feeling that I wasn't alone. Cautiously, I turned around looking toward Ashley Drive, and for a second couldn't believe what I saw in front of me. I was almost completely surrounded by hundreds of wharf rats! Instinctively, I reached for my revolver. I stood there, my eyes locked in on slanted gleaming green eyes that seemed frozen on me—their next meal. At that moment, the police radio blared out, startling the rats that scattered in every direction.

*

Jailbreaks were common. Not all municipal and county facilities were rated as maximum security simply because those serving time were there for relatively minor offenses. There were, however, maximum areas in local facilities that were used to confine felons pending transportation to a state or federal prison facility.

One afternoon, patrolling solo, I headed for the eastern fringe of the city limits to assist the sheriff's department hunt for an escaped prisoner. I entered a working-class neighborhood of single-family homes with larger-than-average yards. Scanning the front yards looking for some sign of life, housewives hanging clothes on the line or small children playing, I was concerned about the potential for a hostage situation if the prisoner was cornered.

I turned onto a dead-end street, driving slowly, following the sound of several dogs barking. The barking took me to the last house on that street. I advised the police radio dispatcher I would be out on foot searching the area. While walking up the driveway toward the carport, two or three small Chihuahuas challenged my right to be on their property. I noticed the rear door to the house in the carport was ajar.

Trying to stay alert to any surprises, such as a fleeing and desperate escaped prisoner, keeping one eye on those pesky little dogs was not working to my advantage.

Finally, one of those little noisy brats nipped me on the leg. Turning to shake him off, I saw a white male bolt from the rear door, heading toward the interstate. I ran after him with a very determined little doggie clamped to my lower leg. I caught the guy, just as he was about to scale the chain-link fence bordering the highway.

I got him by the ass, at the same time, the dog had me by the leg. A sheriff's patrol unit spotted me and came to my aid. The deputy, laughing, grabbed the prisoner who was still determined to escape as yours truly was spitting out expletives no father would want his daughter to hear.

I felt a little sorry for the owner of the dogs. Besides three Chihuahuas, he had two other larger dogs, none with tags. When County Animal Control responded, the owner was cited. What a circus. The dog owner was fined, the prisoner was captured, the deputy got a good laugh, and my leg was sore as hell. I guess the deputy came out on top of this one.

I think over the years I received more dog bites than anyone else in the department. Once, I even had to take rabies shots—not very pleasant.

Terri Elliott & Sassy
TPD—First K-9 Team—1982

15

The Humorous Side of Policing

On the job, humor is definitely therapeutic. The day-in, day-out encounters with human misery take a significant emotional toll on most police officers. Humor has a tendency to cushion the more depressive aspects of the job. Thankfully, most cops, if not born possessing a good sense of humor, will develop one along the way. It's a matter of emotional survival.

*

Routinely, the administrative personnel would order a take-out lunch, and someone would pick up lunches for a dozen employees. Sometimes, one or both the patrol division's administrative officers would use a staff car to pick up the lunch order. One day, Lou and Larry went together to a drive-in restaurant. Just as they were leaving, a convertible full of young women in bikinis pulled alongside the officers to ask directions.

Larry zealously exited the car from the passenger side, leaned into the convertible, and began conversing with the young ladies. Lou couldn't see them from his perspective, so he inched the car forward, craning his neck to get a better view.

In the meantime, Larry, after giving directions, trying to be debonair, moved toward the police car to get back in the front passenger seat. However, his eyes were still on the ladies, so with a big smile, he reached and opened the back door, got in, and closed the door, which of course can only be opened from the outside. Seeing Lou looking back at him, Larry realized he'd locked himself in the backseat, and the ladies were watching.

Thinking quickly, he blurted out, "Well, come on, driver! Let's go! Let's go!" By this time, it was a toss up as to who was laughing the loudest—Lou or the ladies in the convertible. Larry didn't laugh. Instead, he was very red-faced.

*

Escaping embarrassment is a real skill in police work. In most cases, you're just lucky if you do. Getting off the day shift one Sunday, I decided to hit the department gym and work out with the weights. The gym was on the second floor above the records section, and the workout area was set up on the stage. I was alone, not unusual for a Sunday afternoon.

At that time, I weighed a total of one hundred fifty pounds after a heavy lunch. I started out bench-pressing one hundred thirty pounds, working my way up to one hundred forty pounds. Not bad for a lean guy. Well, some days you seem to be stronger than others. This was, I thought, one of those days. Wrong!

Feeling my oats, I pressed one hundred fifty pounds on the bench press and felt strong enough to keep going up. As you get older, you're supposed to get wiser and know when to quit, but not so this day. I loaded up the barbell with one hundred seventy pounds.

In a hurry and anxious to break any of my previous amateur records, I did not slide the locking collars on the barbell to keep the weights in place. On the bench, I started my lift, straining to get the one hundred seventy pounds up and realized it wasn't going to happen. Before I could reset the barbell on the stand, my right arm weakened, dropped, and the barbell dipped to the right, causing all three weights to slide off the end of the barbell. The eighty-five pounds on the left side immediately dipped down, allowing all those weights to slide off. All six weights bounced off the stage onto the main floor of the gym and rolled around like loose pocket change.

My first thought was of the personnel working in the records section just below the gym on the first floor. I grabbed my towel and keys, leaped off the stage, and headed for the far-end exit door, which was closest to the locker room. Entering the locker room, I heard running footsteps and voices at the opposite end of the gym just across the hall door leading downstairs.

*

Some Tampa old-timers will readily remember the Azalea Lounge. Nicknamed the Flower Pot, and later just referred to as the Pot, it was located one block over from the police department building on Tampa Street.

It wasn't unusual to relax with a drink on Friday afternoons, waiting for the paychecks to arrive from City Hall, but it came alive after the evening shift. Once the vice team was off, we all mingled and played the pinball and shuffleboard machines.

One night, about a dozen off-duty officers and I were all sitting at the bar when several members of the vice squad walked in. The few tables were already filled up when a young black man entered and walked right up to a long-haired, hippie-looking guy, an undercover cop.

Our seedy-looking friend offered to sell the undercover officer some marijuana. The officer acted gleeful and asked if some of his buddies at the bar could buy some too. Needless to say, the salesman was dancing all the way to the rear parking lot with several plainclothes cops in tow.

The officers had him in a semicircle behind his car as he rummaged through his trunk. With a song on his lips, he turned around with a big grin on his face and an armful of marijuana. His grin folded loudly enough to be heard when he turned around and observed shiny police badges held out by the smiling cops.

*

186

One of the downtown walking beats was home to an all-female fashion college. Keeping in mind the greatest majority of police officers are honest, ethical, trustworthy, and dedicated to do the right thing, I'll refer to the next character in uniform as *Sneaky*.

Sneaky was assigned to the walking beat on the midnight shift. It was suspected at the time by a number of his fellow squad men that he was spying on the college students. It seemed that from a particular alleyway, one could see some of them inside their bedroom windows on the second floor. They were obviously unaware of their visual vulnerability.

Several officers decided it was time for a surveillance of Sneaky. Sure enough, there he was in the alley, prepared with binoculars no less. Knowing Sneaky would deny the deed, other members of his squad came up with a scheme that would leave no doubt in anyone's mind what he was really up to. Unbeknownst to Sneaky, he was about to reveal all his dastardly deed upon returning to the police station at the end of his tour of duty.

When Sneaky walked into the muster room, he was accused of peeping on the girls. He denied it, of course, and also denied owning binoculars. At this point, the other officers were laughing hysterically, telling him to look in the mirror. From a distance, he looked as if he was wearing a pair of black-rimmed glasses.

It seems that the night before, his cohorts had gotten into Sneaky's locker and dabbed the ridge on the eye ports of his black metal binoculars with black fingerprint powder. You might say another case was solved by the use of fingerprint powder. Its use may have been somewhat unconventional, but nevertheless instrumental in solving the case.

*

When it comes to good cops, Buz Sawyer is right there on the list; not only was he a good cop and later a detective, he retired as assistant police chief of Tampa.

When Buz was assigned to the Homicide Bureau in the detective division, he flew to New York City to interview a possible homicide suspect the FBI had in custody.

Right from the get-go, everything turned to shit for Buz on the New York trip. First, because of a bomb threat at the UN, there was no FBI agent to meet Buz at the airport. Being resourceful, however, he managed to work his way via train and subway to the general area of his destination.

Once out on the street level, he looked around in awe, not having any idea where he was. He spotted a beat officer and thinking he was in luck, approached him, identified himself as a Tampa police detective, and asked for directions. Buz said the cop spoke so quickly in the typical New York manner that he didn't understand a word of the directions he was given.

Perplexed, he asked the officer, "Could you repeat that?" The beat officer retorted, "Fuck you. I told you once."

Just his luck, that last bit was the only thing Buz could understand. "Well, fuck you too," replied Buz. He later said that was definitely his first and last trip to the Big Apple.

*

On 1979, Captain W. A. "Buz" Sawyer and I, Division Commander Joe Pelkington, were assigned to attend the Police Use of Deadly Force Policy Seminar at Northwestern University in Evanston, Illinois, just north of Chicago.

The first night we were there, we decided to take the fifteen-minute train trip to Chicago, found a restaurant, and sat down by a window that gave us a great view. While enjoying cocktails, we observed a large crowd of what appeared to be demonstrators in front of a building across the street. Whatever the event, it was well covered by the news media. There were TV cameras all over the place.

We learned from our waitress that the building was City Hall. After dinner, we walked across the street. Feeling pretty good after a few drinks, we decided to play to the TV cameras, hoping our colleagues back in Tampa would see us. We put our arms on each other's shoulders, smiled, and waved at the cameras.

After a few minutes, we learned why the crowd was there. This was a *gay rights* demonstration. We both broke out in cold sweat. Just our luck—they would see us on TV back home. We figured that now was a good time to down a few more drinks. No one back home mentioned it, and we never said anything to anybody about it until many years later.

*

One midnight shift, Officer D. J. Halligan and I checked out an unmarked car because no marked patrol cars were available. Occasionally, the sergeant would authorize an unmarked car if we wanted to be unobtrusive, hunting for burglars as we did on this occasion.

This particular night, we started our surveillance in Sulfur Springs and pulled into the Floriland Mall on Florida Avenue, parking dead center in the lot. Our car was concealed not only by darkness of night, but we were also shadowed by mall stores.

Anyone traversing Florida Avenue could not spot us. While sitting with coffee, we spotted Franz Warner cruising up and down Florida Avenue in his marked police car. You could hear one of these late 1960s cars a pretty good distance away in the quiet of night. When you gunned it, it had a unique sound of its own.

Franz was a young officer not too long off probation, patrolling on his own. He was well motivated and flew from one end of his patrol zone to the other all night long, checking buildings and suspicious persons.

A short time later, back in the car, D. J. looked over at me—I was driving. We both chuckled, and when Franz passed us driving north on Florida Avenue, I peeled out of the parking lot with no headlights on, squealing tires.

D. J. said, "He's spotted us and is turning around." We were both laughing because Franz thought he had himself a burglar or, at the very least, a reckless driving case. I ripped across Florida Avenue and turned west on Hamiller Avenue. By this time, Franz was on the police radio advising the dispatcher he was in a chase. He gained on us more quickly than we had anticipated.

D. J. yelled, "Turn right! Turn right!" Instinctively I turned. Now I was heading north; but to our surprise, in our haste to lose Franz, we turned on the wrong street and ran right into a dead end. In the meantime, Franz told the dispatcher he had the suspect's car cornered. Then the dispatcher called us to back up Franz.

"Shit!" said D. J. "I didn't think about that."

I grabbed the radio just as Franz pulled up behind us with his overhead emergency lights on. I told the dispatcher, "We're 10-97 [on the scene] with zone 20. We're right behind him. Everything's 10-4. We don't need any more units. Don't send any more units."

Franz looked back expecting to see us.

I yelled out, "My mistake Franz, I meant right in front of you."

Franz was speechless for a moment and then blurted out, "What the fuck are you two doing?"

We couldn't answer him because we were laughing so hard at the profane way he asked the question. I had never before heard him use profanity, which is a rarity in this business.

Needless to say, in the middle of the night with the radio calling us, we were pretty loud.

A resident heard us, popped his head out his bedroom window, and said, "I really don't give a shit what you're doing, but would you please do it somewhere else?"

*

A new officer, Jamie Hunter, was assigned to me for training. Jamie was a former schoolteacher, so I believed that gave him somewhat of an advantage on this job. And it did. Jamie was well above average in intelligence and possessed a good sense of humor.

It was a Friday on the evening shift, Jamie's first night on the street. No sooner were we in the cruiser when we received our first call—an aggravated battery in a trailer park on Himes Avenue near Cypress Street.

When we pulled up, a small group of trailer dwellers were witnessing a man and his wife fighting just outside their house trailer. Upon approach, we observed blood on both.

The wife, several front teeth gone, was yelling profanities at her husband; he, in turn, yelled right back. I separated the two, motioning for Jamie to take the female into the trailer while I questioned the husband outside. The pair reeked of alcohol and both needed a bath and mouthwash.

Just as Jamie cleared the doorway with the wife, the husband began fighting with me. I wrestled him to the ground, and Jamie came running out to assist me. While we were in the process of handcuffing the guy, the wife charged out of the trailer, screaming, "You fucking cops, leave my husband alone!" taking a feeble attempt to land a blow on Jamie's face. He stepped back in surprise.

I yelled, "Grab her, and get her on the ground."

He did, but ended up in a tussle with her before I could secure Pa Kettle and help handcuff Ma Kettle. I told Jamie to get on the radio and call for the paddy wagon.

Clearing that call, we noted that we both had bloodstains on our uniforms, and the night was just starting. Jamie caught his breath, collecting his thoughts, then asked, "How often do you get into these situations?" I said, "Oh, not too often. Maybe four or five times a night."

Remember the times when you wished you had a camera to catch something on film that may never happen again? This was one of those times for me.

Jamie's eyes practically exploded, he turned in the passenger seat to look directly at me, mouth agape, and said, "WHAT?"

"Yeah," I said, "and sometimes you just have to shoot them before they shoot you. And believe me, when that happens, the paperwork takes all night."

I burst out laughing, and Jamie paused, then laughed—realizing I was joking at the expense of his newfound career.

*

The next night was even more exciting. At roll call on Jamie's second night, the sergeant handed me a warrant for battery. To my surprise, the warrant was for a Mr. Thompson, a man I knew who lived several blocks north of my own home. I had met him one day while jogging.

The neighborhood, although inside the city limits, was primarily rural with scattered fields, older small homes, warehouses, and other commercial buildings. Mr. Thompson lived in an old wood-framed farmhouse adjacent to a large field owned by one of the local utility companies.

The field was used to store utility poles. From time to time, you could see Mr. Thompson unloading poles from a flatbed truck and stacking them in a neat pile. It takes a pretty big guy to pick up one of those poles, place it on his shoulder, and walk away. Mr. Thompson was bigger than the average big man—about six foot seven and not an ounce of fat anywhere on him.

At times, when I patrolled this area, I would stop at home for lunch and drive by Mr. Thompson's place, and we'd talk. He was very respectful, enjoyed talking, had a good sense of humor, and a great disposition. I pondered on the best way to handle the situation. Knowing he wouldn't give an officer any resistance, I knew he would come along without a problem. But I thought about it on the way out and decided, without informing Jamie, that all I had to do was tell Mr. Thompson to just go down to the booking desk the next morning and they would process him and he'd be released until court time.

I decided to have some fun with Jamie, though. As we approached the Thompson house, Jamie realized how close it was to my home and commented on it. I said, "Yeah, I know this guy and he may be trouble. He's already served time for manslaughter and has a bad temper."

I drove up in front of Thompson's house. I purposely made my approach, so Jamie would be the one making the first contact with Mr. Thompson. Before Jamie could get out of the cruiser, Thompson walked right up to the passenger side. Jamie was already nervous, but then the man leaned forward, placing his left hand on the rear door, and his right hand on the front fender. His entire head and chest covered Jamie's opened window.

By this time, Jamie's chest was pulsating rapidly and his eyes couldn't open any wider. I told Thompson that I had a warrant for his arrest. He just laughed and went on to make general conversation. Jamie looked first at me then at Thompson as if he was wondering *what the hell is going on here?*

Finally, I asked Thompson in an impatient, aggressive tone, "Well, what's it going to be?" Unbeknownst to Jamie, a wink from me signaled Thompson to play along. "Do you want to cooperate or does Jamie have to wrestle your big ass into the backseat?"

Jamie looked over at me, mouth agape again, and he was absolutely speechless. At that point, Thompson and I both broke out in laughter. Jamie breathed a silent sigh of relief and melted back into the car seat with an expression on his face that said, "Thank God." Just before driving off, I told Thompson to report to the booking desk the next morning. Like I said, humor on this job is healthy.

*

One night, the patrol district office man said, "Hey, Captain Joe, a lady just turned in one of our portable radios. She said it fell off the back of the paddy wagon down on skid row when the officer drove off." I introduced myself to the elderly lady, thanking her for her honesty and for bringing us the radio.

When an officer was assigned to the paddy wagon, he was usually very busy running from one end of the city to the other, picking up arrested subjects from patrol units. Because officers frequently were out of the paddy wagon on a scene and out of earshot from the base radio in the wagon, they checked out portable radios, monitoring for calls.

On this night, Officer George Tiller was assigned to the paddy wagon, and the log indicated he had checked out the portable the lady had retuned to us. I instructed the office man to contact Tiller and have him report to my office but not to mention the found portable radio. At this point, I guessed Tiller was frantically trying to backtrack and find that radio.

When approximately thirty minutes had passed and Tiller had not yet entered my office, it reinforced my guess that he was still trying to locate somebody on skid row that may have had some knowledge about the missing radio. I inquired on the shift commander's radio as to where he was and when he expected to arrive at my office, but there was silence.

When he responded on his base radio, I detected by the roar of the paddy wagon engine that he was moving quickly. He assured me he would be in my office shortly. When he arrived, he desperately attempted to conceal his anxiety, with little success.

Not mentioning the portable radio, I engaged him in general conversation with inquiries such as, "Busy out there tonight? I guess you've been running all over town."

Tiller's responses came with obvious nervousness. I could visualize his mind wandering back to skid row, trying to figure out where the radio might have fallen off the rear running board of the wagon. I guessed he was having visions of some drunk going from bar to bar trying to sell it. Back then, the cost of one of those portable radios—three to four hundred dollars—was a lot of money.

The more I engaged him in conversation it became clear to me that he was about to break. I couldn't hold my serious posture much longer, and he detected I was stalling.

Finally, right in the middle of saying something to me he blurted out, "DAMN IT, CAPTAIN! TELL ME YOU HAVE THAT PORTABLE RADIO!"

I burst out laughing, as did the office man. Needless to say, Tiller thereafter was seen with a portable radio appropriately hooked to his gun belt.

*

A two-man patrol unit received a fight call to a local bar in their patrol zone. Upon arrival, they separated two guys exchanging blows. Both were bloody nosed and angry. One of the contestants followed the officers' orders to step back and stop fighting, while his opponent refused to settle down. After a reasonable number of attempts to calm this guy down, the officers stepped in. The guy then got physical with the officers, who in turn muscled him down after a minute of grappling with him.

Still catching his breath, he was placed in the backseat of the patrol car, where the officers finally learned his name that he was from New York City and this was his first visit to Tampa.

When the officer radioed for the paddy wagon, the guy sat up in the backseat and loudly blurted out, "WHAT! You're going to arrest me?"

"Yeah," said one of the officers. "What did you expect?"

Very much upset over the situation, he stated, "Damn it, that's not fair. In New York, the cops either beat your ass or put you in jail, but not both!"

*

In another situation, two officers were wrestling with a guy who was pretty much on the intoxicated side. While he was physically resisting and cussing the officers, he was not doing anything to assault or intentionally injure them. He just wasn't eager to go to the Cross Bar Hotel.

Finally, the guy got tired and gave up. He was placed in the backseat but wasn't handcuffed. The officers got in the cruiser; and while they radioed for the paddy wagon, the prisoner, still catching his breath, leaned forward, extending his hand between them, handing them an empty soda bottle, and stated, "You guys are going to get your fucking heads bashed in if you're not more careful."

*

Burglaries are a primary concern on the midnight shift. But midnights can be quiet, and the human nocturnal cadence does not usually take kindly to being up in the wee hours of the morning. During the 1960s, patrol officers still had to wear their uniform hats, even while patrolling in the cruiser. One tactic often used to appear awake and alert while you napped as your partner was driving was to prop your head up with the nightstick. With one end of the stick resting on the car seat between your legs, you rested your chin on both hands, which were cupped over the other end of the nightstick. Then you pinched the leather edge of your hat in between the car door (window) frame and the rolled-up car window. (This held your hat in an upright position, giving the appearance of being awake and alert when actually you were snoozing.) You had to have a partner, however, who'd be skillful in waking you if a commander happened by or if by chance there was a real emergency to deal with.

One night, a patrol unit turned down an alley just east of Nebraska Avenue. The driver spotted two subjects bolt from the rear door of a business and yelled to his partner who, though startled, jumped out and pursued them on foot. The driver radioed for a backup and then joined his partner in the foot chase.

The closest patrol unit was the sergeant who pulled into the alley behind the officers' patrol car. Both car doors were open and the headlights were on. In a moment, both officers returned empty-handed to their cruiser and began to explain to the sergeant what they spotted.

The sergeant listened, but as he departed, he pointed to the police cruiser's opened passenger side door with the hat, just hanging there in the rolled-up car door window and said, "I really don't want to know why that hat is there like that. I think I know, just don't tell me," and he walked away.

*

My partner, Pete Hopkins, was driving while we patrolled the downtown area. The downtown car was the only one in the city equipped with a cage between the front and backseats to transport prisoners. While the back doors opened readily from the outside, once inside, a prisoner could not exit.

After taking a robbery call, we drove to Tampa and Fortune streets. Using the police call box, my partner called the station to place a pickup to broadcast information on the robbery suspects. While he was calling, I looked west across Tampa Street and observed a drunk working his way east toward us. As he came closer, I thought he would soon recognize the cruiser and detour into an alley. But he proceeded directly to Tampa Street, crossed the street, opened the back door of the cruiser, got in, closed the door, and said, "Take me to the Ohio Bar."

I flipped on the dome light and looked at him through the cage.

He looked at me, realized where he was, and said, "Oh, shit, this ain't no taxi," and reached for the door handle that didn't exist. He went nuts and screamed all the way to the booking desk, yelling, "Not fair. Not fair."

*

It's not too often a presiding judge is caught laughing at witness testimony. Back in the 1960s, city court (Tampa) tried cases involving minor law violations, such as city ordinances and also traffic court.

Sergeant Stokes had arrested a man for a minor violation; the arrest took place at night. After Sergeant Stokes testified, the defendant's attorney challenged his ability to see at night.

Believing he could nullify the sergeant's testimony, the attorney challenged him by sardonically posing the following question: "Just how far can you see at night, Sergeant Stokes?"

Now Sergeant Stokes was always in quiet control of himself, never speaking hastily. The sergeant paused as if to think over the question, and the attorney's body language said, "Gotcha."

Just then, the sergeant looked up and said, "Well, I can see the moon at night. How far is that?"

The judge looked at the attorney with a wry smile. Gotcha.

*

An officer we'll call Hollowhead had just a few short years on the street as a patrolman and was constantly driving his sergeant nuts. Hollowhead was assigned to the walking beat in Ybor City, located east of downtown Tampa.

Hollowhead made sure motorists understood that they would be ticketed for parking-meter violations. One day, the shift commander received a call from an officer patrolling the Ybor City area. He advised the commander that he had received complaints about Hollowhead and his issuance of parking tickets. The shift commander interrupted and said, "But Hollowhead is off today."

The officer said, "I know, but he's here in plainclothes with his ticket book hanging out of his Levi's rear pocket. He's hiding behind buildings, staking out parking meters, and issuing tickets to violators."

The shift commander was not a happy person. Neither was Hollowhead's sergeant when he returned to work after his days off. He disciplined Hollowhead with a written reprimand.

But Hollowhead wasn't through just yet. At roll call one night, information was disseminated that the small private Peter O' Knight

Airport on Davis Island, just south of downtown Tampa, would be closed to "normal" air traffic and related business. Hollowhead was patrolling that area.

Later that evening, the shift commander received a phone call from the Peter O' Knight Air Tower. "Err, Captain, one of your officers is refusing to allow a small plane to land on the runway. The plane is in trouble and must land or it will crash!"

The captain paused and then said, "How can he stop a plane from landing?"

The air controller stated, "He's circling the runway in his patrol car, siren blaring, emergency lights flashing."

The captain alerted Hollowhead's sergeant, who was heard speaking into his radio in a quiet but frustrated tone: "Hollowhead, leave the f—g plane alone."

The plane was finally allowed to land, but Hollowhead was not finished. His sergeant arrived at Peter O' Knight Airport just in time to witness Hollowhead chasing the small plane down the runway, siren blaring, emergency lights flashing, advising the dispatcher he was trying to stop the plane for a traffic violation!

Hollowhead's police career was very short.

*

Tampa was recognized as the eighth largest seaport in the nation, so it wasn't uncommon for U.S. Navy ships to dock in Tampa for shore leave.

And where do sailors go on shore leave? There must have been at least twelve bars on skid row and in the surrounding downtown area. It was standard practice to have a shore patrol (military) police officer ride with the downtown patrol car when sailors were on shore leave. Sailors were going to get drunk, rolled by the locals, and get into fights. There was no way our booking and jail facility could accommodate the naval fleet, and we didn't like the idea of locking up GIs anyway; so when we came across a sailor in deep shit or about to get in it, we picked him up and transported him back to his ship.

On the first night of this particular shore leave, we proceeded to the docked ship and picked up the shore patrolman assigned to ride with us downtown. He was friendly and talkative, not very tall, of Italian descent, and we learned, very Catholic. He was excited to be riding with us and jumped into the backseat.

He must have been fairly new at military police work because any war stories we told were somewhat of a shock to him. But the best was yet to come for him this night.

Meanwhile, I told the joke about a guy golfing in a remote countryside village: He loses his ball and while looking for it, he meets a witch who gives him a potion that she claims will enhance his golf game. It does, but then it wears off. He goes back, finds the witch, and wants another dose of the potion. The witch says, "Okay, but I've got another potion that's good for your sex life." Being impatient, he said, "No, no, I don't need that, I'm doing pretty good for a priest in a small town without a car."

Our Catholic sailor shook his head, saying, "Oh no, no, no, that's really bad." We didn't make any points with that one.

As we cruised along skid row and the downtown area, we got out and handled a few incidents involving sailors and locals, but nothing serious.

When the zone 4 patrol car called to meet us at our mutual patrol border, we automatically became suspicious because it was fairly quiet. This meant that the guys were becoming mischievous and were dreaming up funny things to do to the bordering zone car.

I headed for the rendezvous point on Adamo Drive. We approached cautiously, expecting something to happen. We spotted the zone 4 car, no headlights on, back off the road on the dark side of a gas station parking area. This was not really unusual because we liked to be out of sight when meeting. I pulled up parallel, driver's side to driver's side.

Officer Walt Ames was driving the zone 4 car and as we pulled up, he grinned.

We were alert and I said, "Well, Walt, what's happening?"

"Oh, not much, Joe," and just then, a cherry bomb was headed my way. I saw it in time to raise my arm to deflect it, and it bounced off my arm and dropped in between the door sash and prisoner cage frame. It fell into the backseat with our very wide-eyed sailor friend who was now trying desperately to get the back door open, but of course, there were no handles for prisoners to make an escape.

My partner covered his ears and I covered mine, but I could still hear the sailor's words, "Oh, fuck. Oh, fuck."

Then—*bang*. As the smoke cleared, the sailor said in a very quiet, stoic tone, "Take me back to my ship."

I said, "But . . ."

He cut me off. "Take me back to my ship."

All the way to the ship, we heard not a peep from our passenger—he just sat there, lock jawed and wide eyed. So much for police-military relations.

16

Treasure Island's Finest*

Growing up on Long Island, New York, the waters of the Atlantic Ocean at Coney Island, Rockaway, and Jones Beaches were never warm. Even in the hot month of August, the water was always cold. My first dive into the Gulf of Mexico along the beaches of Pinellas County was a reverse shock. I never believed ocean waters could be that warm. I recall weekends in the mid-1950s stretched out on the white sands of gulf beaches soaking up the sun. The deep blue-green gulf waters always fascinated me—so clean, so pure. Who would have guessed more than thirty years later I would be the police chief in the beautiful gulf beach community of Treasure Island?

Retiring from the Tampa Police Department in 1985, I had four job offers: two corporate security positions, an executive director for a police union, and the police chief's position in a small city just southeast of the Tampa Bay area.

The chief's position was the most interesting for obvious reasons. However, the political turmoil in that city at the time was raging, and they were going through police chiefs and city managers like New Yorkers through a subway turnstile at rush hour.

So I accepted the security director position with Lincoln Properties Corporation for the new luxury hotel on Harbor Island in Tampa. While I considered other job offers, Lincoln Properties upped the salary offer. The hotel industry was quite an experience. I worked with a team of other department heads six to seven days a week, ten to twelve hours a day to prepare for the hotel opening.

Starting with virtually nothing, I recruited and trained nine people for security officer positions, formulated safety and security policies, procedures and rules of conduct, a performance guideline, manual, and trained the entire staff about security and safety.

One day, about a year or so after I had retired from the department, my former secretary at the Tampa Police Department, Linda Ambraz, and her husband, Tampa Police Sergeant Pete Ambraz, met me at the hotel for lunch. Linda's loyalty as a police secretary and especially as my secretary was fierce. Lord help anyone who was critical of me, Pete, or the police department. She was outspoken almost to a fault. At my retirement ceremony, I said, "To pay Linda for her loyalty would bankrupt City Hall."

They both knew where my heart was, and that I would jump at the chance to get back into police work. After lunch, they handed me a page from a law enforcement periodical that was advertising for a police chief in the city of Treasure Island. I was chosen and started my new position on March 18, 1987. I never forgot Linda's loyalty and Pete's dedication to the job. When I reminisce, there will always be fond and grateful memories of Pete and Linda.

*

The Treasure Island Police Department's staff consisted of the chief, a lieutenant, four sergeants, one detective, and thirteen patrol officers, including one assigned to marine patrol. The civilian support members consisted of four full-time police dispatchers, one part-time dispatcher, and a police secretary. The lieutenant, who had been on the department for many years, was apparently led to believe he would be selected to replace the retiring chief. He was, of course, very disappointed. For several years before he retired, our relationship was rocky at times. I believe that while he liked me personally, he had a difficult time accepting the way I managed the department.

*

I was well aware that having shifted from a larger police organization, I had to anticipate an adjustment in management practices. I was in for a bigger surprise than I realized. Early on, my problem was personnel issues on a scale that demanded and occupied a considerable amount of time to resolve.

Though I solved a number of police personnel problems early on, there was still much to be done. There were a number of members who just couldn't conform to the job and continued to either be incompetent or simply be disruptive in the work environment.

As the new chief, my recommendation and request to go outside the department to seek out competent first-line police supervisors (sergeants) was not acceptable to my boss—the city manager. Although he was both tough and supportive in many ways and always had the guts to stand up to those who politically tried to undermine the police department, we disagreed on this fundamental issue.

These restrictions left me no choice but to fill sergeant vacancies with candidates from within the department. Several promotions amounted to recycling one incompetent sergeant for another. This was truly unfortunate because at that time, I had access to experienced potential candidates retiring from other law enforcement agencies that would have hired on and been outstanding patrol sergeants. As a result, inefficiency prevailed, and poor supervision on the street exacerbated the problem. Those officers wanting to be true law enforcement professionals often became discouraged or frustrated, and some who had been recently hired resigned and joined other local police agencies.

In hindsight, it always seems easy to retrace your decisions, beating yourself on the head for not being more forceful in your convictions and sticking to your guns. Maybe I could have convinced my boss to seek better supervisory candidates outside the department. Keep in mind—organizational cultures are not always easy to change. While there were a number of dedicated officers on the job, several officers, including sergeants, were generating internal unrest.

The typical malcontents, no matter what the circumstances, were always pissed off about something. This generally spills over and hinders the police operation or at the very least, disrupts the work environment. Nothing was ever right about the police department, yet they always managed to pick up their paychecks every week. The hostility was blatant. There was animosity between members and the lieutenant, members and the city manager, members and city commissioners.

Efforts taken to improve the situation were met with resistance; any inquiry by supervisors about officer conduct or performance was also met with resistance; and many members refused to discuss anything without their union representative. I respected an officer's right to have representation when the issue could have resulted in punitive disciplinary measures. However, some officers were erroneously led to believe they weren't required to answer any questions posed by management about any issue connected to their position as police officers. That misconception was quickly dispelled.

When Sergeant Keith Reynolds was promoted to lieutenant, he took the initiative and dealt with these time-consuming personnel problems. Eventually, most of the malcontents and misfits, seeing the handwriting on the wall, resigned. Others had to be discharged for various and valid reasons.

*

One of the most important managerial tools for a chief is a manual establishing set of rules, regulations, procedures, policies, and professional conduct standards. I was in total disbelief to learn the police department had no organized, well-documented operational manual. There was just a dog-eared pack of about ten pages stapled together that reflected word for word rules and regulations of the St. Petersburg Police Department.

I dedicated approximately eighteen months, mostly at home in the evenings and on weekends on a standard typewriter, developing and organizing a three- or four-hundred-page operations manual.

In the meantime, I issued several directives, outlining key rules and standards. I was not a popular guy with many members because I forbade accepting free coffee, half-priced food, or any form of gratuities. Accepting free coffee and reduced cost food seemed to have been at least tolerated by past administrations, and this was not an uncommon practice in many agencies.

I always believed some in the business community felt obligated to provide discounts to the police. When this became prohibited, I think some folks breathed a sigh of relief. There had to have been a false perception that officers expected these favors and if not provided, it would create animosities. It must have been easier to provide the discounts than be mentally plagued with visions of resentful police officers.

Leaving the station two Friday evenings consecutively, I observed boxes of merchandise in the lobby. I instructed a supervisor to make contact with the generous merchants and express our appreciation but to tell them department standards prohibited accepting gratuities. To some officers, as chief, I was a real bastard. So be it.

Lunching frequently at a local restaurant, I paid full price and left a good tip, but then I learned the price of the coffee was left off the check. Approaching the check-out counter one afternoon after enjoying lunch, I was told it had been paid for by a local bar owner who had just left the restaurant.

I called the man, thanking him but said that henceforth I could no longer accept such favors. Not too long afterward, it happened again. This time, I called and insisted that this was not acceptable. He was obviously disturbed, but grudgingly claimed he understood. However, the man never spoke to me again.

I was especially suspicious of bar owners who were generous to the police. While there are some very fine and honest people in that business, law enforcement and liquor establishments are often on opposing sides of many legal issues, and frequently, the police must enforce laws affecting the bar-and-lounge business.

It took a while for both police officers and local merchants to understand and accept the standard I set concerning gratuities.

There may be a few business people in any community who have ulterior motives for providing officers with gratuities, but most of them understand the reason why they can't be accepted, and I know they appreciate those standards.

*

Shortly after I came to the job, I was confronted by some issues with political overtones. Of course, some individuals in the community had a stake in the outcome of these problems.

First futile attempt to kiss the new chief's ass: One local businessman recently cited for a violation came to my office, introduced himself, and immediately made a complaint about the unfairness of being cited. He wore tailored jeans and a long sleeve aqua satin shirt with pearl buttons. His hair was thick and black, including his chest hair of which he was obviously very proud. He wore several heavy gold chains around his neck. He walked into my office, chest puffed up, with a determined I-better-get-what-I-want attitude.

I listened to his disenchantment with the police department's zeal for enforcing what he described as stupid laws. When he could not read any convincing body language favoring his complaint and detecting that his pleas were not reaping the intended sympathy from me, he quickly changed tactics.

He said, "Listen, Chief, I know coming over from Tampa you're probably looking to buy or rent a home close by. Well, I have this house on the water just outside the city limits and it's available."

I responded, "For sale or rent?"

"Oh, don't worry about that, Joe!" (Wow, he didn't waste much time getting to a first-name basis.) He continued, "The house is just sitting there, and I don't want to sell it and really don't want to be bothered renting, so it's yours for as long as you want it."

I couldn't control myself. I smiled and said, "Mr. Jacobs,* you seem to be an astute businessman. You impress me as a man who's been there and done it all and not necessarily altogether from a legal or ethical standpoint."

His eyes widened just a little, and his lower jaw dropped. I continued, "Only because you don't know me are you free to leave this office with a smidgen of dignity."

Another incident involved Scoop, who worked for the weekly Treasure Island paper. This paper passed through so many different hands so frequently, almost on a quarterly basis, that for all I know Scoop could have even been the owner for a while. He interviewed me for an introduction to the new chief piece for the paper.

Next, he invited me out to lunch at one of the local sandwich shops. After we ordered, he excused himself, returning in a moment accompanied by another man. Scoop introduced this guy as a former city commissioner.

The ex-commissioner sat down and began his tirade of complaints against the police department, the city manager, and the state prosecutors. Just about the time he was preparing to tell me why he had been arrested, I interrupted and asked, "How many times have you been arrested for DUI?"

In the meantime, Scoop decided it was time for him to depart, but I stopped him and said, "You set this up, Scoop. Now I want you to hear what I have to say so you can relay to this community just what kind of police chief they're getting."

Scoop was now uncomfortable but remained seated. The former commissioner, on the other hand, was up and trying to reiterate his complaint.

Before he could repeat himself, I made it very clear I had no control over his previous problem with the city government. However, any future encounters he might experience with Treasure Island Police would cause me concern only if the officers were not professional in the way they handcuffed him and placed him into custody. End of conversation, end of lunch.

While I had made it perfectly clear from the beginning that no one was above the law, I found no evidence of widespread departmental practices of exempting anyone from arrest. In fact, the arrest of this former commissioner for drunk driving and my several encounters with other city officials with other complaints left me with a favorable impression. But it was important for all officers, officials, business folks, and the community as a whole to understand that politicians, city managers, police officers (including police chiefs), family members, and business people were not exempt from the law.

Did I even expect officers to write traffic citations to other police officers for minor traffic violations? Yes. Would they? Probably not. Realistically, that's a professional courtesy we can argue about forever. When men and women lay it all on the line without hesitation, it's extremely difficult to get a fellow officer to write that ticket.

*

One summer, state-level government agencies were very concerned about a water shortage. They requested that local police agencies crack down on the watering ban law. Far too many citizens were ignoring it during the dry season, creating an even more dangerous shortage.

One night, I received a call from a patrol sergeant. He said that while one of our officers was issuing a resident an ordinance violation because his sprinklers were on, his neighbor's sprinkler system came on as well, and of course, that homeowner also had to be cited.

The sergeant's dilemma was that the officer had advised him that the second violator was the mayor. I responded, "Well, why are you calling me? You understand my policy, don't you?"

"Yes, but you know . . . the mayor. I mean . . ."

"Sergeant, I expect you to do your job. If someone is violating the law and a warning is appropriate, then so be it. But there are times when we must enforce the law. I suggest you have the officer do what you know is right. I expect a copy of the citation you issue to the mayor on my desk when I get in to work tomorrow or a written report signed by you explaining why he wasn't cited. Any other questions?"

"No, sir."

The mayor, from what I was told, went ballistic when he received the citation. He asked, "Why are you giving me a fucking citation? I'm the mayor."

I forewarned the city manager when I reviewed the copy of the citation. He responded, "Well, if he violated the law, so be it."

*

This next episode made the local news, and my officers received compliments for their professionalism. The day before I left to attend a management seminar in Orlando, I stopped by the sergeants' office, where the off going and oncoming officers were gathered for shift change. I expressed my confidence in their diligence to perform their duties in a professional manner even though I would be away for several days.

The next morning, while I was enjoying a cup of coffee before the seminar began, I was paged by the department. I called the office and learned they had, in fact, understood my confidence in them. I was informed they had arrested the county sheriff's second in command for driving under the influence, and several officers were apprehensive about what my reaction would be. However, upon my return, I expressed my support for their actions and thanked them for being professionals.

In another incident, an officer on his beat issued several parking tickets one Saturday afternoon after receiving complaints about illegal parking. Not long after that, he was dispatched to the home of the city commissioner who represented that neighborhood—Sunset Beach.

You have to be familiar with this area of town to appreciate the lack of adequate space for parking, especially on weekends. When the officer arrived at the commissioner's home, he was chastised for issuing the tickets. It seems that those who received them were either friends of the commissioner or had access to him and had complained.

The commissioner told the officer, "I'm on the city's finance committee. If all you guys have to do is write parking tickets, maybe I should see what I can do to cut the police department's budget."

Arriving to work Monday morning, I reviewed the officer's memo describing the commissioner's admonishment. I called the commissioner and told him his actions were in violation of the city charter. He had inappropriately reprimanded the officer, who had been appropriately performing his official duties by issuing parking tickets based on complaints. I suggested that in the future he communicate any concerns or complaints he had of police service, including officer performance and conduct, directly to either the city manager or me.

The commissioner stated again that if officers had nothing better to do than issue parking tickets, then he, as a member of the city's finance committee, would do whatever he could to cut the police department's budget.

I acknowledged his intent and requested a copy of his final recommendation, so I could provide the city manager with the level of police service that would be cut commensurate with the commissioner's budget cut.

The budget cut never materialized.

In time, however, and after several further discussions, this commissioner actually became a strong supporter of the police department.

*

While professional ethics and other law enforcement principles are the same in any size agency, the chief in a smaller agency has the opportunity to interact more frequently with citizens than his or her counterpart in larger agencies. In fact, the smaller the agency, the more the chief must be readily available for citizens as well as department members.

In larger cities, when an officer issues a traffic citation to a violator, the odds are that he or she will never see that person again. But officers in small towns issue citations to people they will most likely see over and over again and, in many cases, with whom they are on a first-name basis.

In attending civic association meetings over the years, residents often related stories to me involving police officers who they identified by name. They even gave assessments of certain named officers.

One officer with the reputation of being insensitive was well-known and disliked by not only residents and business persons, but by city politicians.

When I happened to mention to the city manager the possibility that this guy might be one of the few candidates who passed the sergeant's exam and that he might have to be considered for promotion, he just stared at me in a moment of silence, then said, "Joe, I would have to be in a coma before I would let you promote him to sergeant."

The point of all this is that in a small community, the officers and their mannerisms, personalities, and opinions are imprinted on a great many citizens who, in one way or another, become familiar with them.

Conversely, the small-town troublemakers, drunks, and criminals are well-known by officers too. "We found Mr. Rubber Knees staggering home again last night and drove him home" or "Mr. Smith's dog was running loose, and we picked him up" are statements often made by officers in small towns.

Speaking of dogs, I was on the way to work one day in my first week as chief when I heard the dispatcher assign patrol units to a complaint about a dog running loose. After monitoring the police radio and listening to officers chattering back and forth about chasing the dog, I finally picked up the radio and directed them to leave the dog alone and go back in service. There was a moment of silence, then "Okay, Chief." As I arrived at the station, the lieutenant was standing out front.

With a chuckle, he motioned toward the rear of the building and pointed to a rather obvious dog kennel. He then opened the trunk of a police cruiser to display the hoops used to capture and restrain dogs. Not only did officers round them up, it seems that we fed them too and sought the owners out, turning their pets over to them with a caveat that the next time the dog was found running loose they might be fined.

Years later, detectives Kathi Lovelace and Dave Schilt devised a mug (photo) album for pets. We took photos of resident's pets, mostly dogs and placed them in the mug book free of charge. If animals were found running loose, we'd use the photos in an attempt to identify the pet and notify the owner.

After advertising this pet service on the city's Web site and to the various neighborhood civic group presidents, with times and dates that we would be setting up in their respective areas, we had a significant turnout from the residential pet owners. Most pet lovers responded with dogs and some cats. When one called with a boa constrictor, I asked humorously if his legless friend had any tattoos, scars, or any other physical characteristics to distinguish him or her from other boas. He laughed and said, "Just how many people in the neighborhood do you think have boas as pets?"

This is one of many services small-town policing provides its citizens. The city Web site also informed citizens that the police would watch their homes while they were out of town on vacations or business trips lasting more than a weekend. Patrol units checked the homes at least twice weekly. Inspections were conducted on foot around the premises, any and all security breaks or suspicious circumstances investigated.

In the event officers found damaged doors or other access points, the city's public works department would be asked to make temporary security measures. Owners would be notified by phone of the circumstances, including any police action taken. Upon return to their homes, residents could request and receive a copy of the police report involving the home-watch inspections.

People in small towns find it very convenient to call upon the police department for assistance for any problem not provided for by any other governmental agency. And if it is doable, it's done. For example, somebody's air-conditioning unit was too loud, and the police took a noise meter reading at 3:00 AM.

Some requests are humorous. A man complained to City Hall about the sand on the beach being too soft to walk in. Another time, a small aluminum boat had tipped over after midnight in John's Pass, which accesses the Gulf of Mexico; and the boaters in the water were yelling for help. A call came in from a condo adjacent to John's Pass, and the caller stated, "Will you get somebody out here to help these goddamn boaters? They've been keeping us awake for over an hour screaming for help."

Another caller phoned the police and complained about somebody's pet monkey caged in the backyard. He stated the monkey would scream loudly every time a bird flew into the yard. A sergeant talking to the complainant asked the standard questions—name, address, etc. When the complainant provided the location of the monkey and then his own address, the sergeant pondered this for a moment then stated, "But your house is nowhere near the house with the monkey. How can that be bothering you?"

The caller stated, "That's true. I'm down the street a block or two away, and it's not bothering me, but it's got to be bothering somebody!"

Yet another incident involved midnight shift officers charging a man for possessing a large snook (game fish) he caught out of season. The sergeant, a temperamental individual, approached me, stating the fish was already dead when they made the arrest and hinted it shouldn't be thrown out; his officers could clean and share it. I agreed there was no point wasting such a large and good-tasting fish. As I turned and walked toward my office, I said, "Clean it up and donate it to the Salvation Army for the homeless."

I could feel the knives plunging into my back. I didn't turn to see the officer's reaction because I didn't want to be faced with charging anyone with insubordination for shooting the chief the bird.

*

Sadly, there are those incidents that leave a lifelong imprint on the minds and in the hearts of police officers. In many cases, it's a child's demise or a fallen officer that remains hidden inside an officer for life.

While the gulf beaches are beautiful, that beauty can quickly turn ugly when tragedy strikes. On Saturday, June 7, 1998, patrol received a call of an eight-year-old black male missing from the beach. Officers were on the scene very quickly, and other beachgoers were already lined up, organized and combing the shallow waters, shuffling their feet along the bottom.

The mixed emotions in this case was about hoping to find the boy alive, but in reality, even if he was found in the water, too much time had passed; we knew that if found, he would be dead. It wasn't until the next day that the boy's body was found in shallow water not far from the last place he had been seen alive.

The parents, a military family, were, of course, devastated. We all stood by the dock behind the police station waiting for the police boat bringing the boy's body in.

As the boat approached, the father turned to me, understandably emotionally upset. I placed my arms around him and said, "This is going to be a tough one for you." Through his crying, he managed to acknowledge what I said. We provided the family the privacy to be with their deceased son on the police boat. I'd like to believe it helped a little.

I observed that one of my newer officers became emotional over this loss. This case was especially heartbreaking. Such a young boy and a very likeable family, and they were obviously very close.

The officers involved in this case, including myself, attended the memorial service. The family took time to express their genuine appreciation for our efforts in standing by them in their time of grief.

Police officers can feel the anguish of others, strangers or not, by placing themselves in the same position as a person or family in such tragic circumstances. Though they cannot bring back a lost loved one, they can at least let those who are grieving know that they too feel some of that pain.

Our officers routinely gave of themselves in death investigations to the survivors, generally spouses in cases of the elderly, offering assistance beyond the normal investigative practice. For example, an officer would call a day or two after the loss of a spouse or other loved one to see if the police could do anything else to help.

I received a call from one elderly gentleman who had lost his wife the day before. Though he was emotionally upset, he wanted to express his appreciation for the investigating officer's concern, sensitivity, and assistance in a time of need. Unlike officers in larger urban areas, officers in small towns are close to the members of the community, becoming ingrained in the very fabric of community life.

Larger cities are inundated with multicultural issues, and high and violent crime abound so frequently officers cannot take the time to get to know those they serve or offer assistance beyond the traditional police service calls and investigations. The typical patrol shift in large cities is about running from one call to another with very little time between incidents requiring expedient responses to crime scenes, conducting time-consuming investigations.

Another hindrance to trying to work more closely with and getting to know the citizens they serve in large communities is that officers' geographical patrol assignments change frequently.

This negates becoming acquainted with individual neighborhoods. There always seem to be problems with funding community-policing programs.

*

While the extra level of personalized service resulted in success stories, in policing the community traditional police activities prevail; small-town police still need to handle crime in the same manner as their counterparts in larger communities. For instance, Detective Kathi Lovelace recovered hundreds of thousands of dollars worth of property stolen from a local Treasure Island business's warehouse.

Detectives Lovelace and Schilt also solved the crime of an elderly couple robbed at knifepoint by traveling to North Carolina to interrogate the identified suspect. They not only recovered about $7,000 in stolen property and seized evidence for our case on little Treasure Island, but also brought back sufficient evidence they then turned over to one of the county's largest police agencies so they might solve their own cases.

Both of these detectives are outstanding, not only as investigators, but as professional and dedicated police officers. Kathi Lovelace is one of the most effective police investigators I've ever known. Her sphere of knowledge in the fields of police work is second to none. Her expertise and tenacity earned her an award from the Florida Attorney General's Office, an award received by only one or two other individuals in the entire state of Florida.

Detective David Schilt was always ready to do whatever it took to get the job done. With all our ongoing personnel problems, I never received any negative feedback about Dave's attitude. I also cannot recall one bad word he voiced about the police department or city management teams. He always was supportive of both in spite of adverse feelings by his fellow officers. Teaming Dave and Kathi as the department's investigators proved to be an excellent move. They have solved some of the most difficult criminal cases the department ever experienced.

*

Encountering and arresting fugitives in this small beach community is commonplace. Officers patrolling the community regularly respond to suspicious person calls and end up making arrests of fugitives from other states.

Sergeant Dan Morton, capitalizing on information obtained from a citizen, coordinated the search, surveillance, and arrest of a fugitive, which resulted in international news. Sergeant Morton's tenacity and keen sense of police tactics exemplifies that which police organizations strive to employ.

Criminals on the run seem to have a false sense of security in holding up in small communities like Treasure Island.

Officer Vince Marsilia, patrolling on the midnight shift, stopped a traffic violator on Gulf Boulevard. He noticed the driver moving around, trying to either retrieve or hide something, turning to see where Vince was standing. Vince approached on the passenger side of the stopped car, but the driver was still looking for him on the driver's side. Vince peered into the front seat from the open passenger side window, spotting several handguns on the front seat and the driver's hand nearby. He challenged the driver at gunpoint and secured him without any problem.

In the process of conducting his investigation, he learned the man was a suspect wanted in Tampa for murdering and dismembering the victim, tossing body parts into Tampa Bay. He was able to close the case. The elements in this type of traffic stop present the highest potential for officers to be seriously injured or killed.

*

In my eighteen and a half years as police chief in the city of Treasure Island, we only experienced three homicides, all resulting in arrests by Treasure Island detectives and patrol officers. In that same period, there were only about six traffic fatalities. This small community didn't come close to matching larger neighboring cities such as St. Petersburg and Tampa in violent crimes, but proportionately we got our share.

Unfortunately, domestic violence is alive and well in virtually all communities. These crimes take up a substantial amount of time for both patrol officers and detectives. In a typical year, we responded to over three hundred domestic violence calls, yet rarely after numerous arrests were these cases ever prosecuted; the battered victims, mostly women, refuse to bear witness against the offender, almost always their husbands or live-in boyfriends.

The business community in Treasure Island had their share of credit card and check fraud crimes too. One detective can focus 100 percent attention on these crimes alone, but all crimes with leads and/or suspects are investigated thoroughly. A good many crime investigations are handled by the patrol officers themselves; they will follow through cases until they are solved or have to be closed administratively.

*Treasure Island's Finest

Police Chief
Tim Casey

Patrol Officers
Phil Bock
Daren Chiaputti
Jonette Demange
David "Dave" Digiore
Robert Gallaway
Kenneth "Ken" Hilland
David "Dave" Persyn and,

In Memory Of
Officer Charles "Chic" Harding

Corporal Officers
Jared Swetnich

Detectives
Kathi Lovelace
David "Dave" Schilt

Communications Officers
Jamie Dunwell
Ashelyn Johnson
Cheriemaria Mainenti
Lori Setzer
Richard Sheppard

Police Secretary
Charlotte Jones

Sergeants
Armand Boudreau
James "Jim" Kennedy
Daniel "Dan" Morton
Keith Reynolds

Records Coordinator
Charles "Chas" Donaldson

Parking Enforcement
John Paulina

Administrative Assistant
Robin Cahill

Police Reserve Officers
Donald Hugh Fetner
John Gannon
John Makholm

TREASURE ISLAND POLICE DEPT

Tim Casey (Current Chief), Author Retired Chief

Hector and Jonnette Demange

TIPD Marine Patrol

Dave Digiore   Jared Swetnich   Sgt. Keith Reynolds

Sgt. Digiore, Det Lovelace, Gov. Jeb Bush, Chief Joe

Charles "Chick" Harding
Treasure Island's Home-Grown "Officer Friendly"

17

The Political Minefield

My decision to accept the police chief's position with Treasure Island was in part based on the city charter, which shielded the police chief from political interference. Neither the mayor nor the city commissioners, by law, could interfere in any way with appointed city officials. They did have, and rightfully so, the power to make inquiries and conduct investigations if they felt it was necessary. I, however, worked directly for the individual who hired and fired—the city manager.

The city manager form of government is a benefit because it reduces political interference with appointed officials, including police chiefs. I remember being told several days after I took over the chief's job, that there was pressure on the city manager to hold off hiring me; the reason had to do with politicians and others in the community exerting pressure to place their favorite candidate as chief.

But the city manager, Peter Lombardi, was a strong-willed man who refused to relinquish his executive responsibility, choosing his own people. After all, he was the one elected officials and citizens would hold accountable for providing city services. I didn't envy Peter's position as the city manager dealing directly with the city commission. The two most vulnerable appointed officials in terms of job tenure are the city manager and then the police chief.

If the city of Treasure Island had been a strongly mayoral instead of city managerial form of government, I don't know if I would have survived as the chief. Unlike a police chief appointed by a city manager, it's difficult, if not impossible, to be shielded from or avoid the political arena under a strong mayoral form of government.

To maintain the professional standards of ethical law enforcement, a police chief must be devoid of political ties and must allow no decisions to be influenced by politics. But the reality is that a chief must always factor in what political ramifications his decisions will have on him, the department, police service to the community, and of course, the mayor and/or the city manager. However, this does not suggest a chief should forego his oath and ethical standards for the sake of political calm.

In 1996, Peter resigned after many years as the city manager. This left a political vacuum at the onset of elections. When he resigned, one department head also turned in his letter of resignation but agreed to stay on temporarily as the interim city manager. He was a man with whom I had had a number of run-ins in the past. Before he left, Peter warned me about staying clear of the "political minefield."

*

A recently opened gay lounge created an upheaval among a number of residents in the Sunset Beach neighborhood who refused to accept its existence. It became a nightly chore to police the immediate area of this establishment and answer all the complaints by disenchanted local residents. In some cases, they became absolutely unhinged when observing two males doing what they might have expected to see a male and female doing together.

To further exacerbate the problem, this establishment was the only one with property extending down to the waterline on the beach. Therefore, when the entire beach closed at 1:00 AM and the lounge closed at 2:00 AM, all the drunks and sexed-up patrons swarmed out on the beach to spend the night, doing what drunks and lovers tend to do. The residents closest to the lounge and private beach area demanded through their city commissioner that the police handle the situation by stopping these offensive activities.

The only problem with these demands was that at least some of the activities offensive to local residents violated no local laws. The beach was private at that particular location, and patrons could remain there all day and night if they so desired.

Desperate to satisfy angry voters, the commissioner became more and more exasperated. (The title of local political officials vary from city to city; they're either called commissioners or council men and women.)

The situation was further inflamed when one of the police department malcontents, an officer who to this day is unaware that I know who he is, anonymously provided the commissioner with complaints about the department that were either misleading, false, or had already been resolved. In turn, the commissioner submitted his own written complaints to the city manager based on the anonymous information, and I was instructed to respond in writing to the city manager.

One of the commissioner's letters accused officers of falsifying police reports. My comments amounted to saying this commissioner was wrong regarding hardworking, honest, and courageous men and women who would not have hesitated to lay their lives on the line for anyone, including him and his family.

My response to the allegation of falsifying police reports sent the commissioner off on a rampage. He became more determined than ever to have me fired. I assumed it was because he could not handle anyone challenging his demands and/or his authority.

I learned this commissioner, the mayor, and the interim city manager were, in fact, conspiring to fire me. The mayor (we'll call him Moe; the commissioner, Larry; and the interim city manager, Curly) and Larry made a deal with Curly: if Curly fired me, they would support him for the city manager's position.

I had to assume Curly agreed to this because subsequent to a city commission meeting, I was told that Moe announced that he and Larry wanted to make Curly permanent city manager. The other commissioners, visibly taken back by this information, refused to go along because the city was already in the process of seeking a candidate via a national notice, and resumes were abounding. The not-so-patient Curly, totally pissed off, simply quit.

Enter Fred Turner, the personnel director, who reluctantly acted as the interim city manager. This man stood tall. No amount of persuasion from Larry and Moe could convince him to fire me. He knew it was wrong and stood his ground. But as Dad used to humorously say, the plot thickens: Moe had a heart attack and was forced to retire, and Larry subsequently campaigned for mayor and was elected.

When the new city manager came on board in early 1997, I strongly suspected the new mayor would pressure him into replacing me as the police chief. In fact, it didn't take long for the city manager to suggest that I retire. He repeatedly remarked that I didn't have the leadership qualities for the "new" Treasure Island.

Finally, I had had enough bullshit, and I challenged him to inform me in writing, exactly what he wanted in terms of police service for the "new" Treasure Island; if I couldn't deliver, I would retire. I then added, "But there isn't anything you or this community want, as it relates to police service, given the current resources, I can't deliver."

He muttered something like, "Yes, I could give you something in writing."

It never happened. Toward the end of that year, the issue of my retirement waned. I asked the city manager at several of our monthly meetings if he was satisfied with the way I was managing the police department, and he responded that yes he was. In fact, for the following year, he constantly praised me verbally for good work.

Each time I briefed the city manager of the progress Lieutenant Reynolds and I were making with some ongoing personnel problems, he acknowledged and supported our actions.

In spite of resolving a number of personnel problems, there remained ongoing incompetent supervision by at least one sergeant. Additionally, there was police misconduct on the part of another sergeant, and there were also several chronic malcontents who just refused to conform to performance expectations, resulting in a number of resignations and dismissals.

The city's policy for members leaving the department gave them the opportunity to have an exit interview, complete a questionnaire and voice their personal comments about the department operation, and submit them to the city's personnel or city manager's office. I repeatedly requested copies of those exit interviews. Any criticism is information to consider for improving the work environment, management techniques, and general quality of police service. However, it was also not uncommon for employees leaving under conditions reflecting poorly on them to blast the chief, lieutenant, and the sergeants on their exit interviews, placing blame on the boss and others for their problems.

When I asked the personnel director for copies of the exit interviews, he told me the city manager had them. When I made the same request to the city manager, he put me off. I smelled a rat! I had to believe the obvious effort to conceal these exit interviews was for a devious purpose.

It was. The city manager in October 1999 approved a 5 percent pay raise for me. Then in November, he handed me my annual performance evaluation. I assumed the one-and-a-half-page document was at least in part based on the exit interviews by disenchanted former department members as well as complaints made by then currently employed malcontents; these were the same problem employees I had been briefing the city manager about all along. He was well aware of all details concerning the disciplinary and dismissal cases, and he had agreed that several of these individuals had no place in our police organization.

At no time did the city manager ever confront me with the critical contents of the exit interviews or any other source of information he used to base his unsupportable appraisal of my performance.

I responded in writing to each and every critical remark in the evaluation. I had credible information that refuted his negative remarks. This man had denigrated me as a leader by attacking my credibility and ethics, all based on false and misleading information.

I was again stunned when I picked up the morning newspaper one day shortly afterward to see my evaluation in print. It was public information; but in all my years in public service, I'd never known of a chief's evaluation being printed unless there was clear evidence supporting allegations of matters such as serious misconduct, corruption, incompetence, or criminal issues.

After my evaluation became public, the city manager ordered me to set up a departmental meeting so he could hear comments about the issues from both sworn and nonsworn members. This was done. The city manager also arranged for several officers under suspension, pending future disciplinary measures, including dismissal, to attend this meeting. Interestingly, the city manager had been, in recent months, briefed about the incompetence of the members he had invited to the meeting; he had agreed at that point that they were not fit for duty.

With the city manager present, I began the meeting by telling the members that I expected them to be candid and not to hold back any concerns or problems they might have. The suspended members, of course, expressed their disagreement with their current employment status. However, I cannot recall one active member voicing any complaint about the department's leadership, management, or assignments.

Detective Dave Schilt asked, "What's all this about a morale problem?"

The tone of that question said it all; there was no department-wide morale problem. During the remainder of this meeting, every question or concern posed to the city manager had to do with employee benefits such as health-insurance costs and improved pension benefits, and had nothing to do with me.

I could only conclude all the hype generated by the malcontents, under fire and facing severe disciplinary action, demotion and/or separation from employment for incompetence, misconduct, and related behavior was the basis for the city manager's evaluation of my performance.

The following day, I received numerous phone calls of support from Treasure Island residents and businessmen and women. I was told various groups had confronted the mayor and city manager in support of me as their police chief. The *St. Petersburg Times* printed comments made by a number of Treasure Island residents, including presidents and other members of civic associations, who voiced their support for me. The media also printed my response to the evaluation. The reporter, Kathy Saunders, who resides on Treasure Island, was very fair in reporting both sides of this conflict. She went to great lengths to obtain accurate information.

The city manager hired a consultant to review the department operation and interview its members. I had no problem with input from a consultant, but after reviewing the consultant's report, I informed the city manager that neither I nor any of my officers were at all impressed with the consultant's study.

Once the consultant submitted his final recommendations, the city manager held a meeting with the personnel director, Fred Turner, and me. One of the consultant's recommendations included eliminating the lieutenant's position or having "two lieutenants on the staff." There was no discussion. The city manager made it clear the existing lieutenant's position would be eliminated.

All the time he was dictating the way it was going to be, I pondered what happened to the management team concept and the staff's input he had preached about when he hosted a management seminar with the city department heads.

He then turned to me and asked if I was willing to continue on without the lieutenant's position. Now I could be wrong on this next point, but I really believe the city manager had me pegged as a dinosaur in my profession and was convinced I would step down rather than accept those conditions. He perceived me as rigid and incapable of changing, preferring to maintain the status quo rather than progressing forward.

I briefly indicated to the city manager I thought it was wrong to eliminate the lieutenant's position and also pointed out the positives of the chief working more closely with the sergeants and officers. As I told him I was willing to move ahead, I detected his disappointment with my positive response. Ironically, I had previously made up my mind to retire if the city manager had called me in and indicated he could not work with me and simply wanted me to leave. His mistake had been in attacking my ethics, integrity, and leadership ability.

Lieutenant Keith Reynolds played a major role in mustering out those members who either lacked the desire or competency to do the job. Faced with eliminating the lieutenant's position, in the city manager's directive to reorganize the department, Lieutenant

Reynolds stood tall. He accepted the consequences and took a leadership role in that reorganization and was then reassigned as a police sergeant.

Without missing a beat, Keith became the cornerstone of training all police personnel in officer safety and self-defense tactics and firearms, as well as doing all the research into firearms and related components for the department. All this was in addition to his primary assignment as a patrol sergeant. Few people would have maintained his can-do attitude and professional demeanor faced with being forced to give up a higher rank.

In the final lap of this political debacle, sixteen or seventeen members of the department, who at that time represented about 75 percent of the department's personnel strength, signed a letter drafted by Detective Kathi Lovelace about their feelings and submitted it to the local newspaper. The comments in the letter included

(1) The term *clique* as used by the consultant (in a negative sense in his report) would be best described as those department members who are working together as a team, hardworking professionals, willing to take tasks and assignments, volunteer for extra shifts, make recommendations, don't abuse sick time, and desire to be the best and strive to solve our cases/complaints in a professional manner.

The letter went on to say,

(2) In every police agency (any business), there are those who don't like the job, don't like the boss and don't like assignments. Bottom line is if you don't like *your job* and you're not happy, maybe another place of employment should be considered.

And also,

(3) We have never lessened the level of service to our citizens. To accomplish this we sacrificed our own schedules and personal

commitments. We assure you this would not have occurred were there a morale problem.

This letter, unsolicited by any managerial faction in the department, defied the contention that the department suffered from low morale and/or that most of the members were disenchanted with the leadership. On the contrary, police performance demonstrated just the opposite. The hardworking members were openly critical of the malcontents.

*

In spite of all the internal strife, the community received quality police service, although there's always plenty of room for improving the quality of personnel and service in any police organization.

Over the course of the tenure of this city manager, about seven years, much was done in support of and for the police department, keeping in mind such support reaped political kudos for those in City Hall, elected and appointed. Once things settled down, I had no problem putting the past behind me, including what I believed was the unfair portrayal of my leadership abilities.

It was time to redirect all our team efforts to serving the community. Once this mess was untangled, my working relationship with the city manager was reignited. The closing statement in my written response to the evaluation reinforces this:

> In any case, we must continue to work toward the improvement of what I see as the quality police service the community receives.

While I consider the entire unpleasant and prolonged episode as ancient history, it is nonetheless worthy of mention in this book. There are far too many organizational and community demands on the police executive to dwell on political misdeeds. Unfortunately, there are times a leader must respond to unsubstantiated political tripe and slanderous allegations. Surviving that, a leader must get on with business or get out of it altogether.

*

The most troubling ongoing issues always involved personnel. I'm not referring to officers and other members doing their jobs and occasionally making mistakes. It was unfortunate that in my situation, far too much time was exhausted on department members who were incompetent, lazy, disgruntled, or just unhappy in their professional and/or personal lives. Attempts to turn people around to productive professionalism require time-consuming efforts, and many times it's all for naught. Ultimately, the problem children either left the service voluntarily or were mustered out.

Serious and repetitive performance and conduct problems eventually resulted in an officer facing dismissal from the job. On the upside, there were just enough good officers on the department before my arrival who were professional, dedicated, and supportive of my policies: Dave Schilt, Chic Harding, Ken Hilland, Kathi Lovelace, and Keith Reynolds.

And they stuck it out, as did others who were hired in the middle of all this disruption. Eventually, we wound up with a professional and dedicated police team.

During my last few years as chief, getting into a cruiser and out on the street was a rarity indeed. Our police team's level of efficiency simply didn't require the chief's presence. If one sergeant wasn't pulling his weight, then the other sergeants were not a bit bashful in reminding him of the *police team.*

In the spring and summer of 2005, Treasure Islanders' were celebrating their fiftieth anniversary. From May through July, including the traditional Fourth of July festivities, an array of events took place, requiring police coverage. Treasure Island is a small place, and cramming thousands of visitors in it created parking, traffic control, and crowd control problems. I decided it would be good idea to be on the street and available if some help was needed. (I even made sure I pocketed my traffic whistle, although I never had the opportunity to use it.)

I rode with Sergeant Armand Boudreau during several nights, including Memorial Day and the Fourth of July. The police radio was active, and there was plenty of communication among street patrol units, officers directing traffic, and the special beach patrol detail.

To maintain ample patrol coverage, patrol units were assigned to the north side and south side of town, weaving through heavy traffic to respond to calls and handle related problems, with the sergeant and another unit patrolling center city. Sergeant Boudreau and I were center city.

On a number of occasions throughout the night, radio transmissions by officers and sergeants indicated a problem. Each time I contemplated reaching for the radio microphone, someone beat me to it and either resolved the issue, volunteered to respond, or said they had already taken care of the situation. I never had a chance to get involved. This occurred each night I was on the street.

On one occasion, close to midnight, one officer, Ken Hilland, advised his sergeant via the police radio that his tour of duty was ending and wanted to know if he was still needed. A patrol sergeant indicated additional help was necessary and Ken, almost cutting the sergeant off, stated, "Just tell me where you need me." Whatever was needed, someone just stepped in and did it. This confirmed to me what I had surmised for quite some time: that this was truly a dedicated police team.

Knowing I was going to announce my intent to retire soon, I felt good that this police team had it together but felt bad that I would no longer be a part of it. The sergeants, conflicts notwithstanding, coordinated and cooperated totally with each other. The officers were always there and ready, and the detectives were always—and I mean always—busy. The civilian support personnel clicked along with the officers. This police team would prevail long after my tenure.

With the anticipation of my departure, there was no question in my mind, nor those I confided in, that a guy named Tim Casey was prepared to take the helm and become the next police chief. That was my recommendation to the city manager, Ralph Stone. Tim had come on board in September of 1996. He came to us with a very impressive police background and experience in just about every aspect of a police organization.

At first I had hesitated when he applied for a patrol officer position. With his credentials, he had much to offer any police organization, and I wondered how long he would stay with us. After at least three interview sessions, I finally hired him.

Before he completed his first year as a probationary patrolman, he was promoted to patrol sergeant with the blessings of just about every officer on the department. As my administrative assistant, his accomplishments and hard work contributed to the improvement of our police operation in every respect.

And I almost didn't hire him.

EPILOGUE

It takes a special person to survive in the law enforcement profession. When all is said and done, for those of us who love this job, we serve for a lifetime and have absolutely no regrets. We hold our heads high, and long after we have retired, we still consider ourselves to be police officers.

There are many great memories but also sad memories of my forty-three years of police service with both the Tampa and Treasure Island police departments. I will think often of those who lost their lives on the job. I take with me into retirement a deep sense of pride, appreciation, love, and respect for every member of both these departments that I have worked with. I consider myself very fortunate to have been in their company.

When I retired from the Tampa Police Department, I was presented with a plaque that was inscribed,

COLONEL JOE PELKINGTON
"A COP'S COP"

To me, there is no greater honor than to be considered a cop's cop by fellow officers. And when I retired from the Treasure Island Police Department, my boss, the city manager, Ralph Stone, one of the best bosses I've ever worked for, presented me with an American flag that he had flown over the city in my honor.

I have no words to describe my gratitude to the residents and business folks of Treasure Island for their great support, not only for the police department in general, but also for me personally as their police chief.

What I said in retirement letters to members of both police departments was important to me. Not only did I want to be remembered as a good street cop, but I also wanted the men and women on the streets to remember me as a commander and chief who never forgot where he started from on the street, working with the best, never wavering or failing to uphold the integrity of my official position, who always put those I served before my own favor, never taking myself seriously but taking my job seriously. Mom, I know you're up there looking down. I sure hope you're smiling.

End Notes

FICTITIOUS NAMES

    STOUT
    PETE HOPKINS
    PREWITT
    SGT HAZE
    RALPH POUNDHAND
    CM
    JA
    JOHN SMITH
    BRENT WATSON
    TOM BAILY
    ED COLLINS
    TOM
    ROGER MORRISON
    BILL BUTTHEAD
    RALPH SLUG
    RONZ
    LOU & LARRY
    JAMIE HUNTER
    MR. THOMPSON
    GEORGE TILLER
    OFFICER HOLLOWHEAD
    MR. JACOBS
    SMITH

Printed in the United States
100045LV00005B/1-123/A

9 781425 792411